# A FAMILY NO MATTER WHAT

Dare to be happy!

Sandrine

# A Family No Matter What

*The Journey to a Beautiful Divorce, Happy Children,
and a Vibrant Life*

Sandrine Perradin

Library of congress Control Number:
IBN-10: 0-692-96361-8
ISBN-13: 978-0-692-96361-6

Back Cover Portrait of Sandrine Perradin by AliveStudios.Com

# FOR

*My children, our next generation*

# Table Of Content

# Acknowledgments

I would like to thank:

My ex-husband David, for being with me on this journey, for giving me the support and answers I needed to write this book. I wish him and his new bride, Meg, happiness.

My dad for his constant support and for believing in me, always.

My friends and family, who have shared my joys, my struggles, my pains, my laughter and my life. It could not be so beautiful without you. A very special thanks to Gil, Steve, Leslie, and Veronique.

All my angels, fairies, and lucky stars for bringing so much color into my life.

And most of all, I want to thank my children, Timo, Liam, and Sienna, for inspiring me to be the best person I can be, and for giving me the courage to live to the fullest. You are my life. I love you.

# Foreword

This is the story of the love of a woman for her children and family. This is my story. I share from the heart my early experiences; the despair, confusion, and relief of ending my marriage; the success of my life with and after divorce: the lessons I learned, the pain, and the happy moments that created the harmonious life we now live as a divorced family. I share the lows — when I lost faith in myself, and the highs — when I discovered what I am made of, and how I found the courage to embrace and stand up for my core values, my children, my family and myself.

The ending of my marriage was one of the most painful periods of my life, yet it was the most profound. I discovered my strengths, my shortcomings, gratitude, and true respect. I learned to trust my heart, to let go, to choose my battles, and to communicate clearly and respectfully during conflicts. I understood that my ex-husband and I would be in each other's lives until the end. I now know that we are a family, no matter what.

And through all of this, I became the person I wanted to become with the life I wanted to live.

As I wrote and revised this manuscript, I decided to refrain from going into the dirt of my marriage. It would create unnecessary hurt to the ones I love, my family. As couples, we all have things that work and things that don't. We all can be at our worst at any given moment, and I didn't wish to paint an ugly face on my ex-husband, the father of my children. He is a good person no matter his shortcomings, and so am I. During those sixteen years of being together, we had our share of love and laughs, and unfortunately, struggles that eventually took over our marriage.

SANDRINE PERRADIN

# Prologue

Feb 2017...

It is my daughter's birthday; she is turning ten. I am taking her and my two boys to the mall, so we can all be with her as she is getting her ears pierced, something she has been anticipating for many years. She then decides that she wants to have sushi for her birthday dinner. I text David, my ex-husband, and tell him to meet us at 6:30 pm at a little sushi place in our small town. As we walk toward the restaurant, I see David and his life partner, Meg, through the window. They are waiting for us to get a table. Big smiles come to us as we get close to them, everyone hugging everyone. We all sit at the table together to celebrate Sienna's birthday. We light candles, have a few drinks, laugh, talk about life, and give her presents. The evening is light-hearted, fun, sincere, and filled with happiness. Three hours later, we part, hugging each other tight, kissing on the cheeks, and telling each other "see you next week" for Liam's choir concert.

# Chapter One

## Tainted Happy Childhood

The vision I created for my own family started with the family I grew up in. That's where I learned about love and trust, about the agony of separation, about how much children need their parents, and parents need their children. I started life in a small village in France. Our commune, Guereins, with a population of roughly five hundred people, is north of Lyon, near the French Alps. There was one elementary school, a post office, a bakery, two hairdressers, a butcher, a small grocery store, and three bars that seem to always be open. There was always someone in there drinking coffee or a glass of wine. The bars were the heart of the village, where people would get together, talk, gossip, connect, play cards, dice, or bocce ball in the summer. In many ways, it was an idyllic place to raise a family. Your parents always ended up knowing everything you were doing, as there were no secrets to be kept. It was a safe and secure environment. My family included my mom, my dad, my brother, and my two sisters. We were just a typical family, in a typical little French village.

However, typical was never again used to describe my family after that dreadful morning: the day my mom died. When it was still dark outside, early in the morning, our family doctor entered the bedroom I shared with my older sister. We were still sleeping. In a very soft and low voice he said that our mom was very sick. We needed to be very quiet and to get dressed. What he did not say was that she was already dead and that she took her own life after battling years of depression, which we children would only find out the truth many years later. We got up, as quiet as the doctor had asked us to be, and got dressed. The next thing I remember, is being at my paternal grandmother's house with my older sister, expecting that my mom would come and get us soon. After a few days there, one afternoon, the front door opened, and I saw my father coming in. I was so happy to see him! I ran toward him, he kneeled down, and the first thing I remember him saying to me was: "Mommy is dead." I was six years old.

I didn't quite understand what he had said. My brain could not process it. He asked me to get my sister, who was in the bathroom, so I ran there and called through the door, "Anne, Anne, Mommy is dead, Mommy is dead." She responded that it was not true. And I said, Yes it is true, Papa just told me. She was trying to come out as quickly as she could, but the door was stuck from the humidity in the house. She was shaking the door to make it open. I suddenly could sense the urgency, the fear in the air. After trying a few times, she finally came out, and we—my father, my grandmother, my sister and I—gathered in my grandfather's office. My brother and my little sister were not with us, as they stayed with other family members. Four children were just too many for most families to take care of. Anne and I were standing on the couch, to be at same height as my dad and my grandmother. I could hear the drumroll in my head, waiting for my father to say something. What was happening? Nothing was making sense, but my body was on alert; it knew something terrible had just happened. I saw his lips moving and eventually his words made it to my ears, and I heard: "Mommy died while she was sleeping." My grandmother was holding my sister, and my dad was holding me. We all cried together, just that one time. Never again. Tears were not allowed in my grandparents' house; tears were for the weak. After that, I never saw a drop out of my grandmother, nor any affection either. She was a stoic, strong woman who survived World War II by herself with two young kids while my grandfather was held prisoner by the Germans. Seeing my grandmother cry, at that moment, felt unreal, and it was the sound of her pain that got my attention. It sounded like she was laughing. Of course, she was not, but it sounded just like that. This is what my mind decided to focus on, instead of feeling the sadness that was crawling into my heart to stay for years to come.

I have very few memories of my mother. I think my brain blocked out almost everything to protect me from the pain, and everyone seemed to be helping me forget about her. She became an untouchable, immaculate subject. No one in the family, our friends, or in the community wanted to talk about her, or her death. Maybe they were concerned about hurting us, but I think they were afraid to let their tears out. No one seemed to know how to process this sad death. Everyone preferred to just try to forget. Yet her death was never forgotten; how could a village of five hundred people forget the woman who killed herself, leaving behind four very young children and a husband who adored her? It always hung above our heads.

It was May 1977 when she said her final goodbye. School was still in session for a few more months, and life had to resume. After days of staying with family, we returned home, and a new chapter started. We tried to pretend that nothing had changed; yet everything did. She was not there, and she left a huge hole in her place. Just a couple of weeks after her death, we were having dinner, and I was filled with questions. I wanted to understand what had just happened. I started to question my dad, who sat on the other end of the table. He started to respond when suddenly my brother screamed from the top of his lungs, "STOPPPP! Never talk about her, ever!" And that's exactly what we did. We just pretended that my mother had never existed and moved on with life without talking about her.

We all learned to mourn her in private, alone, without any witnesses, not even each other. We let the tears flow behind closed doors, where no one could see us, and come out pretending that all was well. I learned to quickly wipe those tears away and put a smile on my face.

Everyone felt much better when I was smiling. No one wanted to see our tears. No one knew how to console us, or maybe they didn't know how to comfort themselves either and could not help us. That silence erased the memories, not just of my mother, but my life prior to her death. My brain hijacked the first six years of my existence and buried them deep somewhere that I don't seem to be able to access. It feels like my life started the day she died.

It was the same for my siblings. We all seemed to have suffered some type of amnesia. All that is left are little Polaroid moments: her bold and loud laugh, the way she put on her pantyhose, the sound of her high heels on the floor, visiting her once at the hospital, and other insignificant details. Those are moments that I have been trying to hold on to, to not completely forget about her.

***

At my mother's funeral, which my siblings and I did not attend, as my father was advised that it would be too traumatic for us, my aunts and uncles approached my dad and talked to him about which family was going to take which children. At that time, it was unusual for a father to raise four young children alone. My brother was ten years old; my sister eight; I was six; and my little sister only two. In astonishment at such an idea, my father calmly but firmly responded that we were his children, and no one was going to take us away from him. That was the last time anyone would ever bring this up. One thing was certain, my father loved us more than anything in the world and taking us away would have been a death sentence to him. We were his life, his compass to go on without his wife.

My dad was always there for us, since we were born. He made sure we were fed, clothed, and had anything we wanted. He was ready to listen if we needed to talk; there was no taboo subject, except my mother. We were his world, his life, and his reason to live. I knew that my dad would be there when I needed him. He was my safety net, my rock. But with my mother's death, I lost the tenderness I needed so badly. I wanted someone to cover me with kisses, to touch me gently, to show me affection. I became acutely aware of how large a role a mother plays in a child's life by the gaping hole left in my heart when my mother passed. But while tenderness was gone, love was not.

My dad had an enormous amount of patience with us. He rarely raised his voice and always had a word of wisdom to share. He worked as a pharmaceutical rep. It was a flexible job, and he was at home when we came back from school. When I was sick, I spent the day with him. I stayed in the back of the car with a pillow, a sleeping bag, and some books. We drove all day and stopped at doctors' offices. Sometimes I stayed in the car and slept while he made his call, and sometimes I went with him, depending on whether my dad thought it would be okay with the doctor. At lunch, he would take me out to a restaurant. One time, as we were eating escargots, one fell off my plate. I tried to pick it up as quickly as possible for fear of ridicule. So my dad told me the story of the flying snail to teach me a lesson. He was at a very nice five-star restaurant for a doctors' conference dinner. Everyone was fancy and well mannered. For dinner, they had escargots, and as my dad was eating them, one of them flew off his plate. Instead of feeling embarrassed, he started to laugh and announced that he had a flying snail, and the whole table started to laugh. He always had a certain way to teach me to laugh at myself and embrace my mistakes, and he never made me feel lesser or ashamed.

I realized just how much my father cared for me one Sunday evening when I was still in elementary school. We were at the cafe, where my dad was playing cards and having a few drinks with his friends. I was sipping my juice. It was getting late, and I wanted to go home. Behaving like a typical kid, I started to nag my dad "Daddy, Daddy, can we go, Daddy, come on, Daddy…." The café owner, a stern woman with short black hair and huge round glasses, was also sitting at the round table playing cards and obviously annoyed at my nagging. At one point, she looked up from her cards and yelled at me. "Would you just stop bothering your father? Just leave him alone."

My dad put his cards down, gave her a look as cold as ice and firmly responded, "Don't you ever talk to my kid this way. If I want my children to bug me, they can. They are my kids. You do not get to tell them what to do with me." And, he went right back to playing cards. That shut her up, and it shut me up too. I knew then, that he always would have my back. He was my papa-bear, and nobody was going to tell him what to do or not do with us.

Children in the village were always part of adults' life. Parents would bring their kids everywhere they went, so we were always around my dad when he went out. Life in the French countryside in the 70's was joyous, fun, and communal. The atmosphere was about having a good time.

There was always something going on to bring the community together. There were bingo days, school performances, parades with floats decorated with flowers and people in costumes. We also had "Light" night, where children carried lit paper lanterns and marched through the streets. Another festival was the "conscrits," where people born in the same year of any decade (1927, 1937, 1947, etc.) would celebrate for three days, with dinners, parades, and fairs. All generations participated and shared in the good times.

My dad was truly an amazing father. We could always count on him, but there was one thing missing; he did not have the feminine touch that I needed so much. He never received tenderness from his parents, and did not know how to give it to us. He would sometimes forget our birthdays or to get us a present for Christmas. He always could be counted on in crises though, but the instinctive tenderness of a parent was something he hadn't learned. Even with his strong love, I still missed the presence of my mother. I remember being so jealous of my friends in elementary school when their moms picked them up at the end of the day, with kisses and hugs, asking how their day was, with a snack waiting for them at home.

I had no idea at that time that the death of my mother was going to help me be the mother I always wanted to have, or that my father was going to be my model for how I would parent my children.

\*\*\*

It was a very normal "un-normal" life in my village. I was just like any other kid, except without a mom. There was always a look of pity in people's eyes when they were talking with me, that seemed to say: "Poor child, you are so unfortunate." That look suffocated me. It was like I was supposed to be the one to be strong, to tell *them* that it was okay, that we were not so sad, that life happens, and that everyone has it hard. But no one ever asked if I had tears to let fall, no one took me in their arms to let them out. Her death made everyone uncomfortable, and they neither let me forget her absence nor be with my pain. I cried behind doors, alone. And if someone surprised me, I would quickly dry my eyes and pretend that everything was okay. I learned to have the best smile ever, as it made people more comfortable. Overall, I was a very happy child, surrounded with laughter and joy, except when the sadness would overwhelm me. Then I would just hide from everyone.

*** 

When I was fourteen, as part of my eighth-grade language program, my classmates and I traveled to Germany for two weeks. We each lived with host families and spent our days with German students. We traveled around the area, visited the Wall that separated the East from the West Germany at that time, saw castles and cities, learned about the history of the region, and attended school with our exchange students. For the first time in my life, I felt I could breathe! Being away from my village was like shedding a thousand pounds from my shoulders. No one there knew who I was; no one knew my history nor my family. When people looked at me, they saw me, not the reflection my mother's death. I was finally able to be me, only me. It was so freeing. I believed then that I could grow out of my mother's shadow. I couldn't do it in my village, but I could do it away from there.

Within the next five years, I went back two times to Germany. Once again with a student program, and once to visit a German friend. During high school, I had to decide what college to attend after graduation and what I wanted to do with my life. My major was in math and literature and I had no clue about future careers. I was just eighteen, and all I could think about was going back to Germany. I loved it there; I loved the way I felt there. I enjoyed discovering a new culture and a new language. Most of all, I learned that I could become whoever I wanted to be. No one was shoving my past down my throat. I did not know what I was going to do there, but that's where I wanted to go. Right at graduation time, in May 1989, I found an ad in the local newspaper for a French family looking for a live-in au-pair near Frankfurt. I showed the ad to my dad, and he told me to go ahead and try, adding, "If you don't like it, you always can come back home."

Knowing that I was allowed to fail gave me the strength and the courage to take risks. I knew that whatever happened, I could return to my father's open arms without judgment.

I sent the host family a letter and got an appointment to visit them in France two months later, while they were visiting their family. The mother was French, from a city just an hour away from my village, and her husband was German. My dad drove me to meet them, and I got the job on the spot. They both worked and needed someone to take care of the children (an eight-year-old boy and a ten-year-old girl) in the afternoons after school. I would also shop and cook for the family, and they would pay for me to go to school every morning to improve my German. Three months later, I was in Roedermark, a small town near Frankfurt, living with a family that was not mine.

It was the first time I'd been on a plane. I was eighteen years old, soon to be nineteen. I was so excited! I could feel the adventure growing in me, and could not wait to arrive and start my new life. The German father picked me up at the Frankfurt Airport. It was a rainy, cold drive to the house, and it suddenly hit me. I had left my family, my country, and my friends. My au-pair host kept babbling about what I had to do the next day, but I only heard noise, as I covered the tears streaming down my face. My excitement vanished; I was sad and felt lonely.

We arrived at their home, met the children, and toured the house. It was late, and I went to bed, crying for my old life. The next day, everything felt different.

I had to make it work. I had to live the dream I envisioned. I had to make it my place, meet people and make friends. And I was determined to have an amazing experience. After my first day of work, I walked down the street of my new town, looking for a light for my cigarette.

I approached this older woman, and after a challenging conversation (I was not yet fluent in German), I finally understood that she did not have any matches, but she invited me to her house to get some. I quickly assessed that she was a good person, she had a very nice energy about her, and I needed to meet people, no matter the age. I followed her to her house a few blocks away. There, she introduced me to her husband, who was having a beer with a friend. The mom invited me to sit and have a drink with them. I could either go back to the house to be in my room alone, or hang out with them. I stayed.

I did not understand much of the conversation, but I got the meaning. We started to talk, and when I told them that my birthday was just a few days away, they invited me to come back to celebrate with champagne. The mom then started to yell someone's name, and two girls about my age came down the stairs to join us. We tried to communicate, me with my little dictionary and everyone using a lot of gestures, smiles, and laughter. It was my second evening in Germany, and I had already met people. From that day on, this family became my best friends, and I became their adopted French girl. I spent almost every evening, and most weekends with them. I met many more friends, discovered new places, and my German was getting better by the day.

Every morning, I went to The Goethe Institute, a school for international students to learn to speak German fluently. I loved being able to communicate in a different language. It was so rewarding to be understood, and to understand others. To me, it was more than knowing foreign words; it was assimilating a culture. I loved my life there and I was fond of German people. They are kind, honest, with no pretense. They like you for who you are and not for what you can do for them.

I lived in Germany during the demolition of the Berlin Wall, coining the infamous saying "Mr. Gorbachev, tear this wall down" speech from President Reagan. It was the end of an oppressive time, and hope for everyone was in the air. I felt it for myself as well, it was a time for transformation.

By June 1990, after ten months there, my life was well anchored. I had my rhythm and my routine. I was happy. I went back home to France, twice during that year, for the holidays. Each time, it felt less and less like the place I wanted to live in. I felt I needed to be away to learn more—to meet new people, to discover life and to grow into the person I knew I could be. I was very happy to see my family and friends in France, but could not wait to go back to Germany, to the life that I chose to create.

# Chapter Two

## America, I Have A Dream

After eight months of living and working in Germany, I had a clearer understanding of who I'd become, who I wanted to be and what I wanted to do. I was ambitious and wanted to make it big, whatever that meant. I thought that a degree in business would get me there. And for that to happen, I had to be fluent in English.

My plan was to find another au-pair job in an English-speaking country. My choices were England and America. England was closer to home, yet I heard stories about how the English treated the au-pair as servants, which did not appeal to me. The United States was so far away. If something did not work out, I couldn't just take my car or a ferry back home, and that scarred me. The thought of being alone on another continent was pushing my comfort zone. I did not know yet, where I should go.

It was May 1990, when I received a letter out of the blue. It was from a high school friend who had moved to Georgia, to get to know the side of her family that moved to the U.S. after World War II. She wrote, "My long-lost cousin in Atlanta needs an au-pair for his family, and I thought of you." She went on to describe the family and the job expectation. "You work from 8 am to 6pm and are free to use their car. Are you interested?" Of course, I was interested! This was exactly what I needed to make up my mind. The fear of going so far away disappeared.

I was going to America... The land of promise, where all dreams come true. And I, Sandrine Perradin, from a small French village, was going to live there. I felt so proud. I was just nineteen. I had no idea how to even visualize the potential of this new life; it was too big to imagine.

I replied to my friend, and sent a letter of reference from my German hosting family, along with a resume. A few weeks later I received a note from the American host, welcoming me to their family, expecting me in late summer. I was going to take care of a two-year-old and a new baby on the way. I left Germany at the end of June and spent the summer in France with my family, preparing for my departure. This time, I was going away for eight months, without short visits home. Moving to the USA was not the same as going to Germany; there were lots of papers to fill out and to be approved. Within sixty days, I got my visa.

Exactly one week before I turned twenty years old, on September 20, 1990, after being in the air for over ten hours, I stepped foot on American soil for the first time. I felt so much happiness to be in America. I wonder if pioneers felt this way? Not knowing what was coming, but ready to embrace life and determined to make it the most it could be.

I was all smiles when I went through immigration. I looked so happy that a custom agent stopped me on my way out, wondering why I was smiling so much. All I could say was, "Because I am in America," grinning from one ear to the other.

The American mom was at the airport waiting for me. She was six months pregnant, with a little girl hanging from her leg. She tried to say my name, butchered it, so right away we both decided that they would nickname me *Sandy* to make thing easier. I was so proud to have an American name. I was ready to be a new person, once again.

The couple and their children welcomed me as one of their own, and I stayed in touch with them for many years afterward. They became my relatives away from France. They introduced me to friends, family, and colleagues. They helped me sign up for college, to study English. They supported my choices, my eagerness to meet new people and to visit new places. I was a young woman wanting to explore life to its fullest, and they approved. All they were concerned about was my safety, and that the kids were taken care of properly.

I cared for the children during the day, and went to school in the evening. I signed up at a junior college, attending English as a Second Language (ESL) classes. To my surprise, my baccalaureate was not fully recognized and I had to take the SAT. It was just one month after I arrived in the country, and it was by far the most difficult test I've had to study for in my entire life. It was in English, and I just did not have the skills yet to understand everything they were asking me. I don't recall my SAT score, and I doubt it was very high, but it didn't matter. I was accepted into school.

There was another au-pair just down the street from the house where I lived. We were in the heart of Atlanta, in Midtown, with old Georgian houses, surrounded by huge trees and parks. It was as safe as it could be for a big Southern city. The au-pair was from France as well, and within a few days of meeting each other with the kids, we became inseparable best friends. We met more foreign people—French, German, Iranian, Dutch, Canadian, Moroccan—who were either au-pairs or students, as well as many Americans. We became each other's family. While our stories were different, we all had one thing in common: we had left our homelands to build a better life, and that made us understand and relate to each other.

English was my second foreign language in high school, and I didn't know much. It was amazing how much energy it took to process what people were saying. Having a conversation was exhausting. I was hearing words in English, translated them into French, thought of the answer in French, and translated back into English. The topic had usually changed by the time I could speak aloud.

I recall the patience and flexibility of my host family, and I thank them for that. They helped me grow; they helped me get better. The mother sometimes asked me to take the car to do an errand. I would get to the destination in twenty minutes, but it would take me two hours to get back. I didn't understand that in Atlanta, the names of the streets changed along the way. This was before GPS in cars and before cellular phones, so for Christmas, I got a map in my stocking.

Grocery shopping was also time consuming. I was never sent there if we needed last minute groceries. It's amazing how long it takes to find a pie crust when you have no idea what a pie crust is. There was a lot of aisles to go through and the products were very different from what we would find in France at the time.

I remember how I was surprised by the food, especially the bread. In the 90s, in Atlanta, it was only Wonder Bread. I missed my baguette. I never got used to the milk, either, especially the 2% kind which tasted like cloudy water. Even after 27 years of living in America, I haven't been able to accustom myself to it. Dinners were also a culture shock. Back in France, every meal is eaten around the table while chatting and talking about life. Everyone starts at the same time and ends at the same time. We never take a plate away unless everyone is done. That first dinner in America was memorable, even traumatic.

We all started around the table at the same time, but one by one, the dad, the kid, the mom finished eating, took their plate and went away. I ended up all alone, with no one to talk to at the dinner table. I swore to myself that I would never eat this way when I had my own family. I would stay French to the core, and do it the way I learned growing up: we would all sit down every night, all together, sharing our days, and excuse ourselves only when everyone was done. But for the time being, I learned to adapt and to eat a little faster so I would not be left alone anymore.

\*\*\*

After six months of living with my American family, going to school and discovering life in Atlanta, my return to France was quickly approaching. I had to figure out what I was going to do next. I had originally planned to go back home and go to college. But I fell in love with America and with the life I built there. I could finally have real conversations in English. I had an amazing group of friends. The American way of life suited me. I was fascinated by the spirit of entrepreneurship and the freedom Americans have, to reinvent themselves, over and over.

Everything was different; everything here was big: the cars, the houses, the roads, the food portions. Heck, even dreams were bigger. I wanted to stay. I didn't want to go back to France. I liked school and life in America, even if I missed certain aspects of my country. I wanted to keep studying at my school and get a bachelor's degree in marketing. I talked to my father, and as always, he was supportive. I got a student visa; my grandfather agreed to sponsor my studies, and my dad and brother were helping me financially as well. My job was to excel at school and stay on the honor roll so I could benefit from a scholarship. I did that.

As a full-time student, I lived in a basement apartment with two French roommates. We were going to the same school a few miles away. I'd drive my brand-new, used Oldsmobile Cutlass '72, my first car. It felt more like a tank, with its deep roaring sound and used a gallon of gas every time I pushed the accelerator. Life was made up of going to school, small jobs like babysitting and waitressing for pocket money, studying, enjoying life with my friends, and making sure my grades were excellent. I graduated from Junior College and moved on to Georgia State University for the last two years of my marketing bachelor. In less than a year of college, my heart felt overly heavy. I was missing my family, my childhood friends, my culture, and my country. A friend of mine was moving back to France, and convinced me to move back with her.

I was seduced by the idea. I sold everything I had, quit school, and moved to Paris at the beginning of the summer 1994. I thought I had it all figured it out. I found an accounting school to attend, thinking that numbers were my thing and found an internship with a big company. I met new people, learned a new job, and had the time of my life partying in the Capital. What I didn't realize, was that all I had needed was a break, a vacation break, but not a life change. After two months, I woke up and realized the mistake I'd made. What was I doing in France, and what in the world was I doing in accounting?

I felt like I was sitting between two chairs, with a love for two countries—my roots and past on one side, my freedom and future on another. France felt so tiny, small-minded, and stuffy. It was too little for my dreams and for whom I'd become. I had learned the American way, and I didn't fit in a French company that was all about hierarchy and not potential. I love France, the culture, the food, my family and friends, but it was very clear that it was not for me, anymore. I guess I had to come back home to truly understand that I did not belong in France, but rather in America.

Right at that time, the mother of my American host family called, saying that she did not understand what I was doing in France. She told me to come back to Atlanta, finish school, and then move back home if I wanted to, but to get my degree first. She offered to let me stay with them, and even asked her brother to get me a job in his company. After a week, I quit my job, packed my car, drove four hours and moved back to my dad's house. He didn't expect my return, I did not call as it was so sudden and so late at night. He saw me with my luggage, and all he said was: Are you hungry? I knew that my dad was always going to be there for me, and support whatever decision I made. He always said: Go, discover the world, live your life, and if you don't like it anymore, you can always come back home. And that's exactly what I did. I stayed home with him until I got all my ducks in a row to be ready to move back to Atlanta.

My grandfather refused to sponsor me this time. He believed that I should not have quit the first time; he didn't trust me anymore. I had to find a way to pay for my college tuition on my own. Once my decision was made to go back to Atlanta, it took me a few more months to sort out my visa. Six months later, I was back in Georgia, living with my American family, working during the day as a receptionist, attending night school, and studying the rest of my free time. I was not going to drop the ball again.

## Chapter Three

## Sparks In His Eyes, Love In My Heart

In September 1996, I graduated with a bachelor's degree in business administration from Georgia State University, and immediately looked for a new job. In March 1997, after many different interviews, I accepted a position as a marketing assistant in Atlanta. It all started with a meeting for a sale's position. The manager believed that I would be bored with the job and thought I would have more fun working for David, the marketing manager, who was also looking for an aide.

When we met, David read my resume and started to talk to me in German, as he had lived there for a few years too. We got along right away, and he hired me as his assistant on the spot. I loved working with him. He was a combination of smarts, creativity, hard work, and a lot of fun. He was driven, and had sparks in his eyes, which looked like as though there was always something cooking in his mind. He was also very funny. We were the perfect team, not just as colleagues but on a personal level as well. We spent eight hours together every day, talking about work and life and ourselves, and we came to appreciate each other.

The more time I spent with him, the more I wanted to be with him. We became close quickly. He was a fascinating person. He seemed to enjoy life to its fullest, be it at work or after hours. He had great friends, was going to music shows, rock climbing, camping, biking, and scuba diving, among so many other things. He was always looking for a way to experience and engage with the world.

After a couple of months working together, we drove from Atlanta to Charleston, North Carolina, for a trade show. It was our first time away together, and the drive was filled with interesting conversations. The more I knew about him, the more attracted I was. This was not primarily physical attraction, though he was a good-looking man—tall, slim, a smile that invited you to smile back and beautiful, sparkling green eyes. There was something else about David. Maybe it was his drive. He was a man with a vision, and he was making things happen. He was committed to moving forward, seeking adventure, always with an idea cooking in the back of his mind. On the way, back to Atlanta, we saw the Hale-Bopp comet crossing the sky for a few seconds, a once in a lifetime sight, and I immediately knew that something very special was cooking for us.

I looked forward to going to work every day. I was learning a lot, and he expected the best out of me. He pushed me to excellence, and knew I could deliver.

He was also fascinated by me. He was intrigued by my open mind, my international background, my thirst for experiences, my creativity, and artistic capacities. I challenged him and kept him interested. He said many times that he never knew what would come out of my mouth. I was one of the most interesting women he'd ever met. And we laughed so much; that was probably one of the biggest assets we both had, the ability to crack each other up. We'd burst into laughing fits, thinking the exact same thing at the same moment. It took just one look and the giggles would start.

He inspired me to move forward, to be bold, courageous, and to see bigger, much bigger. The topics of conversations were endless; there was never a boring moment. I fell in love with him, but of course could not tell him; he was my manager. Two months after we met, in April 1997, as we were playing darts after work, I could not hold back anymore. I turned and walked straight to him, in a very decisive manner, and kissed him. He embraced me and kissed me back passionately, all night. From that evening on, we spent every day and evening together. Only at work, did we have to hide. Employees were forbidden to date each other.

Soon after, the company was downsizing, and ironically, David had to be the one to let me go. I recall the moment perfectly. We were taking a stroll in a park, after a day of work, and he said: I have good news and bad news, which one do you want first? I asked for the good one first. He said, well, we don't have to hide at work anymore. So I looked at him and said: "Ohhh, did they find out?" He said no, so I asked, "Ohhhh, did they fire you?" He said no, and right there, I finally understood what he meant, and his hesitation. And I said: "They are firing ME??"

So many thoughts came at once. How, why? I asked him if it was because they found out about us. No, no one knew, they were just downsizing, and since I was one of the last hired, I was one of the first fired. I left him at the park, needing to be alone, to process what just happened. I went for a walk to figure out what it meant for me.

I only had five months left on my work visa, and then I had to move back to France. You graduate, you get a one-year working authorization, and then you must leave. That's how it was then, when you had a student visa. How could I find another job? Who would ever want to hire me for just a few months? I had no idea what I was going to do; I felt doomed, and I didn't have a plan.

Fortunately, David was able to keep me on at the company as a contractor to help him out. Instead of getting paid, I got a computer. I did that for a month or so, and I was learning to build websites during my free time. I found another temporary job in a printing shop and learned more about graphics. I tried not to think too much about the day I would have to leave the country, which was supposed to be end of December. I just waited to see what life had in store for me.

That summer, David asked me to move in with him. We rented this little basement place in midtown Atlanta. We were so much in love. We had our share of heated conversations, but we knew how to laugh and let go of most of the little things that did not work. I just couldn't imagine life without him, and apparently, he couldn't imagine it either.

\*\*\*

On a Sunday morning, a month or so after we moved in together, as David and I were out for a lovely brunch, he got out of his chair, knelt in front of me and asked me to marry him. I was surprised, as we had only been dating for a short while, but I was so in love with him that I didn't care; I knew that I wanted to spend the rest of my life with him. On September 26, 1997, two days before my twenty-seventh birthday and four months after our first kiss, David and I eloped. It was only him and me, the Justice of the Peace, and the love we had for each other.

We also planned a wedding ceremony and reception that our friends and families could be part of. We kept our elopement secret, afraid that some family members might be upset, and not attend the ceremony scheduled for later in November. David's family arrived a few days before the wedding. My brother, sisters, friends, and cousin flew in from France, and we spent a week together, having a wonderful time. My dad was not able to come. Unfortunately, his health prevented it, so my brother, stepped in to give me away. I received a fax from my dad the morning of our wedding. I could hear his tears through his words because he couldn't be there with me.

Our ceremony was intimate, personal and beautiful. It was held in a concert room just across the street from our apartment. The bridal music was taken from one of David's all-time favorite bands, Phish (the song was a cover of "Also Sprach Zarathustra," also known as the theme song of "2001: A Space Odyssey"). In France, we usually have only one best man and bridesmaid, but in America, there is often a whole flock, and since David was going to have more than one best man, we decided not to choose between our best friends, but instead to have them all on stage with us. They were about ten of them, including my siblings and my cousin, surrounding us with candles. Even our dog, Dakotah, was part of it. When it was time for us to give each other the rings, I heard David whistling, and to my surprise, Dakotah walked up the stairs slowly to the stage toward us and sat down in front of us with the rings around his neck. I was surrounded by all the people I cherished most and by the love of my new husband. I believed that our marriage and our love were going to last forever.

The day after our wedding, David and I left to spend a week in the Florida Keys for our honeymoon. I remember seeing our friends and my family behind the car blowing bubbles, laughing, waving and wishing us happiness and joy. A week later we returned and started to prepare for our move to Glendale, Arizona. David had been accepted at Thunderbird, The

Graduate School of International Management, to pursue his MBA. We packed everything we owned in a twelve-foot long truck and crossed the country. It was, again, the beginning of a new life chapter. David started school, and I ended up getting a job there as well as the webmaster's assistant. We seemed to always find a way to live life next to each other, sharing the same experiences. This place was amazing, with students from all over the world. After a year, I became the webmaster for the school. Our lives were filled with fun, excitement, and challenging work.

Arizona was a growth time for both of us, a major stepping-stone in our careers. David was learning how to become an entrepreneur, as I learned to become an internet consultant. The atmosphere in the school was magical. Eighty percent of the student body were from a foreign country. It was a mixture of cultures, languages, food, and provocative thoughts. Such diversity in one campus. After David graduated in the spring of 1999, we moved back to Atlanta, where he found a job.

Soon after taking that new position, he had a vision about a business and decided to start his own company. After a few false starts, David created a company that recycled cell phones, an industry that did not exist then. He was a visionary, and eventually recognized as the expert by the industry and government. It was beautiful to watch him change the world. No one could stop him, though many tried. Many dismissed him, some laughed at him, and a few big companies saw the potential and stole his idea, leaving him in the dust. But he was resilient. He still could see what others could not. It was challenging, exciting, and very hard on the nerves: A typical entrepreneur's life.

David grew his company while I worked as the lead information architect for a website company in Atlanta. Two years later, IBM recruited me as a wireless business consultant. The concept of wireless was still in its infancy, and very few people except techies knew about it. I was not one of them. The day of the interview, I asked the decision maker why they wanted me, as I knew very little about this technology. His answer stayed with me to this day: "Because you know how to find answers, and that's what we are looking for." He was right; when I had a question (and I always did) I would find the answer, or the people who had it. My mind was always wondering how things worked, and how to make things better, in a very artistic yet logical way.

I spent my days with high-level executives, designing innovative business solutions. I was part of a team that built one of the first wireless applications, even before we knew it would be called an "App." Working there

35

was like being part of the future. My brain loved it; I was always challenged to learn more, and I had a knack for asking the questions that made the executives think and challenge their ways of doing business. Then suddenly, the dot.com bubble burst, and many departments were laid off, including mine. It was just a year after I started working with them, just months after the 9/11 tragedy.

Like so many others, I had to start over. In the eight months that followed the crash, I felt lost. I could not find work in my field, and I had no idea what to do next. I was down and unable to get back on my feet. My heart was darkening, and my tears seemed to be replacing all the joy.

It was a difficult time for David as well. He was seeing me drifting away from life and joy and he did not know how to help. He felt powerless and so did I. In response to my uncertainty with life, a friend of mine introduced me to Siddha Yoga, which is a combination of meditation and chanting. Something incredible happened during one meditation. There was a recording of the guru's message playing for us to listen to, and I felt stroked by a beam of light that went through my whole body. It filled my heart with love, removing the darkness. After a few months of meditation and some time to process where I was in life, I was back on my feet, and determined it was time for a change.

# Chapter Four

## Nesting for Motherhood

**W**hile I enjoyed my work as an internet consultant, I did not want to do that anymore. In the summer of 2002, at thirty-two years old, I knew I needed something more, something different. I had outgrown my love of flying around the US, spending my nights in expensive hotels, and putting in seventy hours of work each week. I wanted more time for me, more time with my husband and friends, and I wanted to visit my family back in France more often. And most of all, I wanted children. I was ready to start a family of my own.

After considering my needs, wants and options, teaching in a private school seemed to make the most sense. There, I would not need to have a teaching degree, as my work experience would suffice, and I'd be working forty hours a week, with all the holiday breaks: Thanksgiving, Christmas, spring break, summer and a few other days in between. That would be the perfect schedule for us. I imagined eventually spending summers in France with my children, surrounded by family. That was my new vision.

It was mid-July, and the school year started in late August. My dad was visiting me for the first time since I arrived in America, twelve years earlier. I told him about my plans and he encouraged me to go for it. While he went for his morning shower, I opened the yellow pages and, one by one, started calling each private school listed in Atlanta. After a few replies of, "No, thank you, we are filled for the school year," I heard: "That would be great; we just had a teacher cancel on us. Can you come today for an interview?" I was so excited to tell my dad what had just happened in the last 20 minutes. That afternoon, I visited Ben Franklin Academy High School. I was hired on the spot as a French and algebra teacher, and I would also act as the internet and marketing manager for the school.

Teaching at Ben Franklin Academy was a transformative experience. The headmaster's vision was different from the typical school program. He believed that every child was capable of learning; it was the system that did not know how to teach well.

That was his core belief, and with the help of an amazing team, he built a successful charter school. It took root in an old Georgian house that was surrounded by beautiful and fragrant rose gardens. Everyone was invited to smell, pick a flower, walk freely around, and pet one of the two cats that were there for the children. Having animals seemed to calm the students and soothe their anxiety. The school started with fewer than twenty kids and had about sixty students when I came on board. It was a very small and caring community. My biggest class was four children. It was a one-on-one education, a mastery program where the teachers had to adapt to the children individually to teach them the way they would learn best. Ben Franklin Academy was known as "the school with rose gardens" in the community, but many parents also nicknamed it "The Last Hope School." Most students came to us struggling and broken from the system, believing they were worthless, never going to graduate. Parents were losing faith, not knowing what to do, hoping that a miracle would happen.

I witnessed many miracles every year. Seeing all those children transforming in front of our eyes in just a few years. During one of the high school graduations, the mother of one of my students embraced me and said with tears of joy and deep gratitude: "You saved my child. You all believed in him, and look at him now.

They said he was not going to read, and he is now graduating from high school on his way to college with a 4.0 GPA. Thank you, thank you, you saved my child." It was the most rewarding job I'd had to that point. What we were doing in this school mattered. We changed lives and had our lives changed too. We learned to be trustworthy, honest, vulnerable, and to respect each other. Students and teachers became a team, working together to build their future and their dream. Little did I know that this job was preparing me to parent my own kids.

Just a few months after I joined the school, I became pregnant with our first child. The school's staff was uber supportive, and the students loved seeing my belly get bigger and bigger. Even before his birth, my baby became part of the school, as everyone witnessed his growth. There was so much love around my baby and me. Being pregnant was everything I had hoped it would be. I was glowing and happy; I was floating on a cloud of love. Sensing the baby moving inside of me was magical. Nothing else seemed to matter. This child filled my heart with pure love. This was like nothing I had ever felt before. How could I already love so much, and I hadn't even met my child?

My aunt from France came visit to be with me for the birth, but sadly missed it. I somehow believed that my child was going to come early, but I was wrong. In fact, the baby was not ready to come out, and showed up two weeks after my due date. I had taken some Lamaze classes with my husband to prepare for the birth; I wanted to deliver the natural way with no drugs. But when the contractions started, I cursed them; none of the teachers said it was going to be the worst physical pain I would ever feel in my life. After many hours of agony, I finally gave up and agreed to an epidural. Once they put that long needle into my back, the pain completely disappeared, and I just waited until the midwife told me to push.

That time came, just a few hours after the shot. I pushed twice, and my wondrous miracle was born. My son, Timo, was born on a summer day in 2003. For the first time, I truly understood the love my father had for us, the depth, and its unconditional nature. The second I became a mother, everything seemed to make sense. There was no fear or pain, only love. I spent hours watching him. That's all I wanted to do. I stayed the next two months at home, in a blissful state. I was blessed with a healthy child, and I loved taking care of him. He was such a happy and healthy baby. When he turned eight weeks old, we went back to France for ten days to show him off to my family. I was so enamored. He was my new love, and he took precedence over anyone else, including my husband, not realizing at the time that I was pushing him away. All that mattered to me was my child, nothing or no one else. I was living for my baby boy. It was pure goodness, pure joy, pure love.

Upon my return from maternity leave, I asked the school to cut back my hours so I could spend more time with my child. When the time to go back to work came, I cried. How could I leave my baby in the care of someone else? Who would care for him the way I could? Who could know him as I knew him? Who could love him as much? No one could, but I had to find the closest thing because I had to go back to work. I found this wonderful granny to take care of him. The first day I left him there, I cried all day at work, wondering what kind of mother I was to leave my son just at two-month-old? I thought I was the most horrible mother on Earth. I made it through the day, and when the bell rang, I could not run fast enough to get my child, to hold him in my arms and smother him with kisses... begging for forgiveness. The next day was still hard, but it got better and better. Granny was taking great care of Timo, and kept a journal every day. I wanted to know how long he slept, how much he ate, if he smiled, if he cooed, and the time he pooped. I was anxious about missing all of his "firsts".

I worked three ten-hour days per week and stayed home the rest of the time. David's company was growing, so I was able to cut back on my working hours. I enjoyed spending all that time with Timo. I cooked his baby food with organic produce, making fine dishes such as lamb and green beans, fish and potatoes, all mashed with crème fraiche, to make it taste wonderful. We spent hours watching birds in the trees, playing in the grass, and tasting everything he could put in his mouth. I was doing art, painting his fingers, letting him draw whatever he wanted. Everything about him was amazing, and every day something changed. He was growing and developing so fast, I never could get enough of him. Even at night, I couldn't wait for him to wake up to nurse, so I could see him one more time, to hold and kiss his sweet little hands and feet. Life seemed as beautiful as it could be.

David was mostly working from home, allowing him to spend time with us, and getting his share of kisses. David and I were learning to become parents, and our couplehood was put on the back burner. I was all about being a mother, slipping away from being a woman, a lover, and a wife to my husband. All I wanted was my child, and I figured my husband could take care of himself, that he did not need me. It took years before I realized that I was killing our marriage, to become a parent. I had never learned to be a couple with children; I never had a role model. My dad was a single dad, and David's parents had been divorced since he was a young child. Neither of us knew how to navigate this new territory, and I let the love of parenting our child take precedence over everything else.

Nine months later, I became pregnant again, but this time was different. While I was extremely happy to be with child, I felt a darkness in my heart, like a gray cloud hovering above my head. I did not understand what was happening. At the time, I was back in France for the summer with my son Timo. When I returned a month later, I went to see the doctor for an ultrasound, and then the sad faces started to turn toward me. The baby was dead. I was two months pregnant. I ran into David's arms and cried. He too was very sad. He appeased my pain by saying we would try for another baby as soon as we could. The doctor suggested that I let my body reject the fetus, but it was not coming out. After a few weeks of having this dead body inside of me, we decided to have the doctor take care of it. Once removed, the sun shined again. I was of course very sad, and spent a few weeks weeping, but the dark cloud of death disappeared.

Two months after my miscarriage, I became pregnant with my second child. Joy filled me again, and the pregnancy was as beautiful as the first one. Having a toddler, and running around with a big belly was the most wonderful thing I could have asked for. More love around me, more joy, more blessings. This new child also had a mind of his own. He did not want to come out, and the doctors suggested inducing me again. I refused, as I just could not start his life by ordering him to come out. It should be his choice, to start life on his own terms. The baby and I were healthy, so I waited longer, and during the last night of August 2005, two weeks after his due date, my baby decided it was time. Once again, I tried to have a natural birth, but after a few hours of unbearable pain, I asked for the epidural. Just a few hours and two pushes later, my second son, Liam, was born.

The doctors looked a little worried about the color of his skin. They wondered if he had enough oxygen as he was born with the cord around his neck. I just wanted my child in my arms. I wanted to nurse him. I told them to give him to me; I knew he was fine, I just knew it, but they did not know. After an hour, they took him to the ER to keep a close eye on him. No one was telling me anything, and no one knew what was going on. After the longest two hours, I demanded to see my baby. They never found anything wrong with him.

The next day, David brought Timo to the hospital to visit us. I was told to introduce Liam to his older brother, and to put him back in the nursery, so Timo would not feel replaced. That's what I did, but to my surprise, Timo had a huge fit. He screamed for his baby brother and wanted him back in his arms to smother him with kisses. Twenty-four hours later, I came back home with our newborn and a two- year-old toddler. Life was busy and wonderful. Liam, like his brother, was very easy, and I was as much in love with him as I was with Timo. I did not know that my heart could hold so much love to share between two little angels. Once Liam was able to sleep through the night, I put his crib into Timo's room, and they share a bedroom to this day.

I cut my working hours a little more and was able to stay at home five days a week. I now was working a twenty-hours part-time. Life outside my children held little interest for me. I preferred staying home with them rather than going out with my husband for live music, or out with friends. Nothing and no one brought me joy the way my boys did. And when I went out, I brought them with me. I wanted to be the best mother I could be. I read everything about their growth, about their health. Their health was my priority, and I wasn't going to let a physician be fully in charge. I challenged them. I knew more about vaccinations than most doctors, and knew all the natural ways to take care of them. I spent nights holding them on my belly when they could not breathe because of a cold, and countless hours soothing them. I wanted to be the only one to do it. I had to be there, be the one who was holding them. I needed it; I needed them. They were growing healthy, strong and joyful.

David and I were very happy parents, but we started to follow different paths. I was focused on the children; David was focused on the company, and I started to lose interest in David's business.

Nine months after Liam was born, I got sick. I did not have any strength, and had to stay in bed for a few days. It was so unusual for me as I was very healthy, eating well and running miles pushing the stroller. I was sure that I had the flu, but for safe measures, I decided to take a pregnancy test; there was one left in my medicine cabinet. Yet, I was sure I was just sick, as I knew exactly the moment I became pregnant with the boys, and this time, it felt completely different.

Well, I was wrong. It was not the flu. I was indeed pregnant. It was a shock to David, as well. We did not plan this new baby, and were not prepared for a third child so soon. I was told as long as I was nursing, the chance of getting pregnant were extremely slim. We were torn between having the baby—and not being able to care for it—or to abort. David wanted some more time, six more months, that's all. After weeks of arguments, and once I realized that I could never abort this child and be happy with the decision, David looked into my eyes, and said: "If this is what you truly want, then we are going to have this baby."

Once the decision was made, we embraced this pregnancy with as much love and wonder as the two others. Once again, I kept working until the day of the delivery. This time, the child decided to come exactly on the due date. And once again, I decided to try natural birth. Sadly, the pain was too intense and I eventually asked for an epidural. The nurse started to prep me, but this baby chose differently and decided to come right away, with no time for the injection. I felt every contraction, one right after the other. Since the midwife believed it was going to take hours, she left to deliver another baby, and I was alone in my room, as I told David I would have plenty of time and that he could go to the Cafeteria to work. When David returned, an hour later, he looked at me puzzled. He kept looking at the machine and at me, the machine and at me and realized that all the contractions were one right after the other and that the baby was coming now. He asked me how I was feeling and I screamed: "The baby is coming out, NOW!!!" I could feel her head coming down, and my body started to push on its own. David ran out the room screaming in the hall of the hospital for a doctor, right now!! The nurse came running, asking me to stop pushing, but I couldn't. The doctor came just in time to catch the baby. And on February 2007, our little girl, Sienna Rose, was born. She was so beautiful, and so much plumper than her brothers. She was already a very healthy baby.

I could not wait to go back home, share her with my boys, and to resume my life as a mother of three. I needed to rest, but the staff always wakes you up every hour to take your vitals, so I left the hospital less than twenty four hours later. We took Sienna with us and went home. I wrapped and swaddled her against my body until she was able to walk. She was everywhere I was, on my body, feeling the beat of my heart. I could smell her skin all day and all night. She slept next to us, so I could nurse.

I reduced my schedule one last time, and was now working ten hours a week. Working with other children did not bring me as much joy, anymore. I wanted to teach my own kids and spend all my time with them.

Timo was thrilled to have a new baby at home. He took Sienna under his wing. Kissing her and caring for her. Liam was just eighteen months old, and he did not like to share his mommy. I had to keep a close eye on him, as he would easily take off, without warning, when something caught his eye. He wasn't afraid to be away from me; he just lived his life, not thinking he might get lost. While Liam was not too excited about the new baby, he was crazy about his big brother. Since he was three months old, they have shared a room. I sometimes just stay behind the door and listen to their conversation. Night is when they bond, sharing their lives.

We quickly nicknamed our baby girl "The Loud Flower," which came from a dream David had on a night when Sienna was just a few months old. He dreamt of being on a TV show where they presented baby animals. The host brought out this creature who was very cute, bold and strong, but was also making a lot of noise. They called it the Loud Flower. As David awoke, he realized that it was Sienna who was making all this noise, while she was sleeping. He's called her The Loud Flower ever since. She is strong, bold, wise, soft, beautiful-hearted, and roars just like that animal in David's dream.

While I was the main caretaker of the children, David was a very loving and present father. He loved spending time with the kids in the backyard, taking them for bike rides, going out camping with the boys, while I stayed with my baby girl at home. He loved them as much as I did, but he also needed a life of his own, outside the children. So, he learned to go on his own, just as I chose to stay home with the children.

# Chapter Five

## Losing My Dad

Sienna was the first girl in the family. My sister had given birth to two boys, my brother one boy, and my dad just could not wait to have a granddaughter. We planned to go to France three months after her birth, in June 2007. I was excited for my dad to meet my daughter. He loved playing with the boys, and I knew that Sienna would charm the heck out of him. She was a calm and smiling baby, absorbing everything around her with big eyes. And she rarely cried.

In April, one month before going to France, the phone rang very early one morning while everyone was asleep. I got up quickly, running to the phone so it would not wake up the children. It was my brother, calling to say that my dad had just died. The cleaning lady found him in his bed, motionless. She called the police and they pronounced him dead. They found a letter next to him addressed to us, children. How could it be? He was fine last time I talked to him, and he was supposed to meet my daughter. I just could not understand what happened. I went back to our bedroom and told David that my dad was dead. He was as shocked as I was. Tears were not flowing, not right away, and once I finally heard the words again in my head, I fell apart. My dad, my hero, my safety net, my number one fan, was gone. Just like that, no warning.

My youngest sister, who was very close to my dad, had suffered an extremely severe stroke two years earlier at the age of thirty. No one was prepared for this tragedy and especially not my father. She was his baby girl. It shattered his heart and left him a broken man. The stroke left her totally disabled. The doctor found that she had a heart tumor and that a piece of it had traveled through the aorta, blocking the passage of oxygen, for so many hours that it destroyed half her brain. In the immediate aftermath, she was like a vegetable on a bed, unable to talk, walk, eat or drink. She seemed gone, yet still alive, trapped in a body that was no longer working. She stayed that way for a couple of months. She slowly re-learned to walk with a cane, still paralyzed on the right side, and she re-learned to eat and tried to talk, but her words were not coming out right. She could not communicate, and her comprehension and short memory were severely damaged. After two years of being at the hospital, she finally came home. Once she returned to my dad's, she spent her days crying, begging for us to terminate her life.

This incident ravaged my dad. He could bear the loss of his wife, the love of his life, because of his love for his children, but seeing his baby girl like that was too much. There is only so much a heart can take. He was tired of so much heartbreak and saw that there was nothing more he could do for her, or for any of us. He was no longer the strong man he once was. He did not have the heart strength to support his daughter this way. He now felt completely useless. His heart was aching, and his body started to fall apart. After years of driving for his job, his back was in constant pain. The doctors told him that eventually he would end up in a wheelchair. He believed he would become a burden for us, and that is the one thing he never wanted for his children. He believed he should be the one to support us, not the other way around. He could no longer endure life; it was too painful.

He had a plan. He put his financial affairs in order, wrote a letter, walked up to his room, swallowed a few pills and was found dead in his bed in the morning. He never got a chance to meet my daughter, and I never got a chance to say goodbye.

His suicide was different from my mother's. My mom took her life as a result of severe depression, at only thirty-four years old, leaving behind four very young children. My dad, on the other hand, had lived his life as best he could, loving us and raising us to adulthood. And then decided that it was time. As my older sister would say, he committed self-euthanasia. He left us a note, telling us that he did not want to become a problem, that we already had our share of burdens.

I understand and respect his decision. I didn't feel abandoned by him or angry by his choice. He was just done. He'd spent his entire life putting us first. We grew up, moved away, had our own families. After his retirement and successfully raising us as a single father, he felt that he was dispensable. The tragic accident of my youngest sister is what finished him.

He was wrong, though, believing that I did not need him anymore. He was still my rock, my person to go to when I felt joy or pain. He always knew what to say when I was down or doubtful. His words of wisdom have followed me all my life, and even today after his death. As I grow as a mother and as a woman, his words still fill me, helping me through my challenges. He is part of who I am. I am my father's daughter.

As my children grow, I understand my father, and respect him even more. I see now how strong he was, but can also imagine the difficulties he faced raising four children on his own. Of course, I wish that he was still here to give me one more word of wisdom, to make me laugh one more time. But my heart knows what he would say, I can hear it, and it soothes me. He is still my role model. If I can give my children the love and devotion my father gave us, then I will consider myself a wonderful mother. He taught me how to be a parent, and how to love my children.

Just as we had been for my father, *my children* became my compass. Being a mother was all I wanted to be at this point. My kids and their needs, became my only priority. No one brought me joy as much as they did. I was giving life; I was loving them like I always wanted to be loved by the mother, I too soon lost. I was raising them with hugs, kisses, smiles, caresses, all the things that I needed when I was little, and I was going to raise them and talk to them the way my father did with us.

Two days after my dad's death, I took Sienna with me and flew back to France to bury him. It was not sad, but a joyful day. We celebrated his life surrounded by his friends and the music he loved. We partied like he loved to celebrate life. I could hear him laughing from above, and being part of this day. As I walked through his house, I still could feel him. I could feel his spirit saying that he was in a much better place and that all the pain was gone. I could feel him happy. And that helped me cope with my loss. My only regret is that he never got to meet my daughter. He would have loved her.

# Chapter Six

## Moving And Growing Apart

Atlanta had welcomed me for eighteen years, and I was filled with many memories and friends, but I knew the time to move was coming. While I loved this town, I wanted a better place for my children to grow. I wanted them to be safe walking or biking. I wanted a great public school system, and Atlanta did not have that. I wanted to live in a village, to be part of a tight community. I considered moving back to France to be close to my family, but one day, as David and I traveled to Boulder, Colorado, to meet his new business partners, I knew we would be moving there. We were walking through the Pearl Street Mall, the main street of Boulder, when something inside me said very loudly: "You are home." It did indeed feel like home.

About six months after this first visit, in April 2008, we moved our family across the country to a small town near Boulder called Louisville. It had great public schools, parks on every corner, friendly and safe neighborhoods, surrounded by trails and nature. And it was nominated the best small city to raise a family in America, by Money Magazine. It was the perfect place to raise our children.

To my surprise, everywhere I went, I seemed to hear someone speaking French. One day, as I was shopping, I met a woman who told me about a group of French ladies who gathered weekly. The next week, I took my kids to the park and introduced myself to the group. Very quickly, I had a big circle of friends. Most of us were French immigrants, with a few Canadians and Americans, speaking French. We shared the experience of being a French person in America, the humor, the food, the language, and the culture. I was able to expose my children to their heritage on a daily basis. I created my own small French village in Colorado. It was the best of two worlds. France in America.

Life was very busy with young children, and a husband growing his business. David was covering the financial front, while I covered the familial front. Looking back, I realize that we never talked explicitly about our roles; we just slipped into them. While it seemed the perfect fit for me to be a stay-at-home mother, I don't think it's what my husband expected from his wife. It was different in the beginning—we were both growing our careers. Now making money was all on his shoulders. To me, it seemed the perfect combination. He was doing what he loved, and I was doing what I loved. I did not realize, or did not want to see, that we started to create two different worlds for ourselves. We drifted apart. Eventually, our two worlds became very obvious; we were no longer living the same life. I was not interested in listening about his business anymore, and he learned to live a life without me.

The flip side of the excitement of being an entrepreneur is the financial instability. We lived a roller coaster financial life. Sometimes we had all the money we needed and more; sometimes we were living on loans from friends and families. The lows created an enormous amount of stress, especially in the last years of our marriage. Money, or the lack of it, was putting a huge pressure on each of us. The more stressed we got, the less we communicated, and the more fights we were having.

We both were trapped in our own fears and started to resent each other. All I could see was how negative and hurtful we were toward each other. It was agonizing for both of us.

I didn't understand what he was going through—the fears of not being able to provide, the fears of not doing right, the fears of failure. He did not share them with me, or maybe he did, but I could not hear them. I, too, was caught in my negativity. I was stuck in the endless anxiety of not being able to provide for my children, and of feeling worthless myself since I was not bringing money home.  It was a never-ending cycle, which probably made David feel more burdened and more afraid himself; and that, in turn, worsened my panic. Little by little, the fights and negativity became suffocating, destroying the love we had for each other.

***

The children were growing, and I realized that soon, within four years, they would all be in school full time. It was time again to think about my next chapter.  I knew that I would want to go back to work again. The question was, what would I want to do? What type of work would allow me to be flexible, and to work mostly from home so I could still be a full-time mom? I was getting ready for a life change. I started to list all the things that I liked, and was good at, and the things I did not like or did not want. I did not want to go back to work 8-5; I did not want to be gone most of the week, traveling. I love asking questions, and I have always enjoyed connecting with people on a deep emotional level.

I seem to have a gift for guiding others to clarity and inspiring them into action, to help create a better life for themselves. It was like I had a special key for opening people's hearts. They tell me their deepest secrets, fears, joys, and emotions. I started to wonder what I could do with that. I researched on the internet and considered therapy, mediation, and coaching. Each of those paths sounded quite interesting; each had pros and cons, but it was coaching that interested me the most. For a few years, David had been working with an ontological coach, and I liked the work he was doing, so I contacted him. His name is Hans Phillips. I wanted to understand what ontology and coaching was about, and if this was something I could truly see myself doing. We spent a few hours on the phone. Hans gave me some homework to learn more about the field, but also about myself, and the choices I wanted to make.

This is how Hans defines ontology: "The study of human beings and our relationship to reality. It reveals your essential nature, when it comes from your core. You realize what you say and hear, shapes your perception of reality. By transforming where you come from, what you say and how you listen, you have a fundamental shift in your life, your work, and your relationship to self and others."

I was fascinated by it. Not just as a job, but also personally. I love it when I can transform myself through the bias of a job. I wanted to know more, and I called Hans to see how I could become a coach. At that time, he was contemplating teaching and training. After a few phones calls, we decided that we would work together. Three months later, January 2, 2011, we started the training. For a whole year, I was part of an amazing group of people, all learning to become coaches. But before we could coach, we had to do the work on ourselves. We had to learn and understand our fears, our core essence, our survival mechanisms, and our cycles of behaviors. It was the most profound work I have ever done on myself. This group learned my deepest fears, shame, ambitions, mood shifts, successes, griefs, joys and life patterns. There were no secrets; it all had to be on display so we could address the roadblocks keeping us from living the life we wanted. We learned how we sabotaged ourselves, learned our strengths and how to create success. The program sessions took place over the phone. We spent six hours together every week, and another twelve hours coaching each other and pro bono clients. Since most of us were either at home with children or working, we scheduled the calls very early in the morning, or late in the evening.

The instruction and the work I did in ontological coaching changed my life–who I was, what I believed about myself, and how I responded to life's challenges. The intense training helped me realize how deeply unhappy I was in my marriage, and how hurtful it was. I thought going through the program might help with my marriage and my relationship with my husband, but instead it showed me the reality I had tried for years to deny.

As a couple, we fought, we talked, we tried counseling, marriage therapy, books, etc... Nothing seemed to help. There was always a little bit of hope when we would get out of sessions, but we'd revert to our normal very quickly. Nothing seemed to change, or maybe no one was able to help us. I tried coaching David, to use the tools I learned, but he did not react well to my teaching him. It had to come from someone else. We could not communicate and be there for each other in a healthy way. It was so frustrating. How was I able to help so many people, yet not able to do that with my husband and my own marriage? I didn't know how to fix us; I was out of options. The only choice I seemed to have was either to accept the way it was, or to stop it. We seemed to have tried everything, but I just could not bear being hurt anymore. We were angry and resentful toward each other. Both of us believed that we were there for each other, and supporting the other the best we could. Yet, we both felt unsupported by the other. As a result, we felt lonely and scared, and mean words were being said too often. Every one of them was like a poisoned arrow going straight into my heart, killing my soul, little by little.

During a spring car trip with the children, we got into another fight. He got out of the car to cool down, and I turned around, telling the kids to be quiet so Daddy would not be upset. And right there, I became conscious of what I truly was doing. Not only was I showing them that it was okay to talk badly to the person we say we love the most, but I was mainly teaching them that it was okay to endure it, and live this way.

That was the turning point for me. I wanted to teach my children how to be happy, kind and caring people, and how to love. That was definitely not what David and I were doing. We had endured the pain for years, and I could have tolerated it much longer, swallowed my tears and my pain and gone on with my day, because of the love I had for him, but I just could not teach that to my children.

It was time to bring joy into our hearts again. Our marriage was destroying our happiness and breaking our family apart. I didn't like the role models we were becoming for our children. I couldn't stand what we were teaching them about marriage, love and relationships. This realization is what finally gave me the courage to admit that our couple was not working, and to find a solution. I was thinking divorce, but I was not quite ready to have that conversation with David. I wanted to give us a last chance. Upon our return home, we talked and decided that we had to change, or call it quits. We tried for a while, but the old selves came back, and the belief or hope that something would change disappeared. We were stuck in our patterns of destruction, both in survival mode instead of in our hearts. We were in our negative selves and only saw the negative in each other.

# Chapter Seven

## The Turning Point With A Vision

**A** few months after our car trip, the children and I went to France to spend the summer with my family. David stayed in the U.S. to take care of his company. He would sometimes join us in France, but this time he did not. We both needed the time apart. I needed to figure out what I wanted to do with my marriage. Having this time alone brought me peace of heart. It felt so good not to have to argue anymore, and to be on my own. Five weeks later, we flew back to Colorado. I was at the airport with the children, on the escalator, ready to meet my husband, who was picking us up. I saw him before he saw us, and all I could think was: "This is not the life I want anymore." At that moment, I knew we were done.

I thought back to a few years after we were married when David and I had bought our first home in Atlanta. I was radiating love and happiness. I was eight months pregnant with our first child, sitting on a bench under an enormous tree, when suddenly a scary thought came to me: *it could all go away.* I said to David, "I want you to promise me that if there comes a time when we are no longer happy together, we have to have the courage to admit it, and quit before we hate each other."

That time had now come. I knew it was time for us to face reality. We were destroying each other, and consequently, we were hurting our children too. Love isn't always enough to make a marriage work. It sure wasn't enough to save ours. We'd been married sixteen years, had three beautiful kids, and it was breaking my heart to think about letting go. It still puzzles me today, how we could love each other so much, and at the same time continue to hurt, and be hurt so badly.

But before I could confront David, I had to answer all the questions living inside me. Was divorce what I really wanted? Was I ready for it? Did I want to take the risk of breaking up my family in the name of happiness? I looked for answers everywhere. I went to therapists, I talked to friends, I read everything I could put my hands on, and it came down to this: No one had the answer but me. Deep down, I knew that I knew the answer; I was simply too afraid to face the truth.

Was I ready to leave, to be the person that "broke the family", to live a life without him, and to take my children away from their dad half the time? No, I was not prepared for that. All I wanted was to go to bed and wake up knowing it was all a bad dream. But every morning, I was back in this reality, and I knew I had a decision to make. I spent about two months trying to gain clarity. I was hurting, and I was hurting David even more now, as I put more distance between us, without telling him what truly was going on. I did not have the words for him yet. Heck, I did not have them for myself.

The fights kept happening, and all I was aching for was stopping this madness. I started to look around for places where I could move with my children. Soon after, a close friend shared with me that she was about to rent her basement. On a Friday evening in September 2012, after another quarrel with my husband, I decided it was time to move out. That was it; I couldn't stay anymore. I had enough. I was going to call my friend the next Monday to tell her I would rent her place for me and the kids.

But when Sunday arrived, I realized that I couldn't take off with the children like that. I knew it wasn't right. If I were to take the kids away from David without notice, it would be starting a war, and I was certain I did not want that. I wanted out, to find peace and happiness, not more ugliness. If I was going to end our marriage, I was going to do it the right way. The big question was: *What was the right way?* I thought about the life I wanted to live after divorce. Until now, all I had been thinking about was how to *end* my marriage. I had to stop thinking about the past and envision my future. How did I want the relationship between David and me to be?

I wanted to be happy again. If I had an angry ex-husband in my life, it would be anything but happy. It would be ugly. I wanted to divorce my husband, but I did not want to fight. My marriage to David was over, but I also knew that my relationship with him would never be over, not with children. We had to change from being a married couple to being a parenting team. The kids loved their daddy, and I would not be a party to destroying him in their eyes. I wanted my children to still have an amazing relationship with their dad; I wanted *them* to see him the way I saw him years ago. I wanted him to be the best daddy he could be. Whether divorced or married, our family would always be my children's family.

While the drive for a happy life gave me the strength and courage to move forward with the idea of divorce, I still had difficult questions to answer:

- What do my children need from me so they can grow strong and happy?
- What are the values I want to teach them?
- Who do I need to be now to support them?
- How can we team up to care, love and be there for them, even with a divorce?
- How am I going to make it financially?
- Where will we live?
- How will I be able to feed my kids?
- What do I need to create this new life?

Of course, I was terrified. While I wanted to believe that we could make it work, I also knew there was a chance that it could become nasty, just like most divorces we had witnessed. It took me a few months to be sure and to build the strength and courage to finally start the divorce. I knew it was going to be one of the most challenging times of my life, and I needed to be ready for it. I had to be strong emotionally, physically, mentally and financially to make it happen.

I wanted the fights to stop, to live apart, but still be there for each other. I wanted us to stay a family. I believed that I would be able to love him again, as a person, if we were no longer together. I wanted what most would say was the impossible. I wanted a Beautiful Divorce.

I did not want an ugly divorce. Our family was already drained from all the resentments, the fights and the constant tension. I longed for peace. I longed for a life filled with love again.

And then, I remembered something that happened twenty-five years before, when I was in my late teens. I observed this couple that seemed to have the perfect relationship. I saw the kindness and respect they showed toward one another. It was the happiest couple I'd ever seen, only to find out later that they were divorced parents! That was how I wanted us to be. They became my role model. If they had done it, then we could too. Every divorced couple around us hated one another, wanted to destroy each other, and wished the worst for the other. Sadly, their children were caught in the middle. My divorce could not be like that. I refused to allow hate to prevail. We were going to be a family, no matter what.

My siblings, aunts, and cousins were all in France. Other than my children, David was my only family here in the U.S., and I wasn't about to let that go. Despite us not getting along anymore, he was still the beautiful man with whom I fell in love, with all his qualities. We all have a positive and a negative side. I wanted to divorce the negative and keep the positive in my heart.

I believed that the impossible could become possible, and that we could transform what everyone expected to be ugly, hurtful and destructive into a respectful, kind, caring, and supportive relationship. That became my vision. I took the lead and was going to make it happen.

I no longer had doubts about the divorce, but how was I going to tell him? I was so afraid. I knew his first response would be anger, and to blame me for what was happening. How could I bear holding all the blame for this divorce, when it was obvious we were in this together?

I needed to somehow create a bubble, a safe space around me to protect me from his reaction, his anger, and his mean words. I needed silence and peace inside my head and my heart, so I could find the strength not to fight back and to react aggressively, as we did in the past. I too would have liked to point a finger at him, and to let him know how much he had hurt me. But we had to stop that destructive cycle. I needed to let go of my anger, my resentment, and my need to be understood.

It didn't matter anymore who did what and who hurt whom or who wanted the divorce. All of the hurting was part of the marriage, and our marriage was over. A new chapter was beginning—and I wanted a beautiful divorced life.

Many difficult emotions surfaced: Anger, grief, sadness, fear, guilt, self-doubt, and also relief. It would have been very easy to get sucked into negative emotions, so it was crucial I stay focused on the future that I wanted to create. I needed to learn how to be the person I wanted to become toward him, and the person I wanted him to be toward me.

The next big question was when would I tell my husband that I wanted to divorce him. It was October. Thanksgiving was coming up, and I could not bear to ruin it for everyone. Christmas was right around the corner, then his birthday, then my daughter's birthday, and then more special days... I couldn't put a dark stain on any of them. There was no right time to tell him, until that day came all on its own.

Early in November we had another fight about my not being supportive of him. It was early evening, the children were in bed, and I knew right then that this was the moment. This time, instead of fighting back and defending myself, I looked at him and said, "You're right. I am sorry. I seem to bring you down and keep you from being happy. I think it is time to put an end to this."

He stopped talking, confused, wondering if I was serious. That wasn't what he expected me to say. Our normal cycle was for me to fight back, to try to prove myself to him, to tell him that he was wrong, and then the tears. I changed the rules by just breaking the cycle. Little by little, he became upset. And as I anticipated, he began pointing a finger, blaming me for the state we were in. I was ready for all of it. I was prepared to not fight back. I looked at him as he threw his angry words, and gently said, "I know, and I am sorry."

This was not the time to highlight his role in our dysfunction, and it was not the time to defend myself. He could not hear. He was trapped in his pain and fear; I knew that my side of the story would surface in time. I let him vent until he ran out of words. When there was nothing more to say, we just looked at each other and went to bed, with heavy hearts and minds.

The morning after I "dropped the D word" on David, was like any other day, but we both knew that everything had changed. That evening, after the kids went to bed, David asked me if I was serious about what I had said the night before. We had threatened each other many times with divorce over the past two years, but this time, we both knew that this was different and our sixteen-year marriage was about to end.

Yes, I meant what I said. We still had love for each other, but we had to stop the hurting. I can't say what went on in David's mind or heart; I didn't have the courage to ask.

After that night, I felt as if I was walking in a fog for nearly a year. I was in a haze until we signed the final divorce papers. I could not wait for each day to be over and to fall asleep so I could escape. Every morning, I woke up realizing "Oh, that's right, this is my life now," with a huge weight on my chest.

As I learned to disengage from the anger, it became easier to talk with David about the divorce in a calm manner. I wondered why this could not have been done while we were still trying to make our marriage work. The only answer that came to me was that I now had the strength because I knew this was going to end, and the fight would be over soon.

We agreed that the next step was to get support, so I found a therapist that I thought could teach us how to divorce. After two sessions, I realized that he wasn't going to help, but rather, he was trying to get us back together. At that moment, I took control of the session.

We were sitting on a couch next to each other, facing the therapist. I turned to David, looked into his eyes, took his hand in mine and said, "We have a choice; we can either have a divorce where we hate each other, badmouthing for years to come, destroying ourselves and our children in the process, like your parents did to you. OR, we can accept that it is our marriage that didn't work: we are still the same good people who fell in love, with the same qualities, and we can leave the bad with the marriage, and keep the good with the divorce."

"What do you want?" I asked, "hate or love, in your life?" I knew his parents' divorce had been hard on him. I also knew how much he loved our children and that he would never want to hurt them, no matter how painful it was for him. And that's what he chose: Love. That was our commitment. It was the last session with that therapist.

From then on, I decided that every word I would say to him and every action I would take, had to answer one question: *Will this lead me to a Beautiful Divorce?*

There were days when I wanted to scream in his face, to tell him to f--- off and tell him how wrong he was, but instead, I asked myself–Was it going to take me to love or to hate? Each time the answer was clear–not easy—but clear.

I learned to breathe and stay calm, rather than reacting out of anger and frustration. I focused on the big vision, not on winning the argument. It's amazing how hard it was to simply breathe and not fight back. Of course, I wanted to curse, to yell back at him, but those twenty seconds of feeling good would have destroyed everything I was trying to build.

By not fighting back, the arguments eventually stopped. I was amazed by how quickly it happened. In a very short time we were able to talk nicely to each other, to laugh again, to hold each other and still have love for each other, even with the impending divorce. We talked like adults: no tantrums, no blame, and no anger—we did lapse into occasional fights. But it was very different than it had been.

As our communication got better, that fact itself brought up a lot of doubts. If we could now communicate in a respectful matter, couldn't we still make it? Did I still want to divorce? Am I making the right decision? Was our relationship as difficult as I remember it being? At times, I believed that maybe there was a chance. But we were still the same people with the same problems that were not going to get resolved.

# Chapter Eight

## Falling Apart

One evening during the divorce process, as I was making dinner, tears streamed down my face. David came into the kitchen, saw me, and asked why I was crying. "Because this is all so sad," I answered. "Well, you wanted this divorce," he said. Yes, I did want the divorce, but that didn't make it less painful. How could he not understand that it was also very difficult for me? When we got married, we had a dream of the perfect happily-ever-after life and of growing old together. I dreamed of a beautiful marriage with him, not a beautiful divorce. And this was the end of that dream. I cried every day from the moment I told David I wanted the divorce. I cried for it all, for sixteen years of life together and all the memories we created.

My life was falling apart, and I was deeply hurt, even if this was what I said I wanted.

I cried when I was driving, when I was taking a shower, when I was watching TV, when I was listening to music, when I was with friends, or when I received a hug. All I needed was someone to take me in their arms and hold me tight and let me cry until I dried out. The only person who could have done that was my husband, but I could not ask him. I stayed strong and happy as much as I could, but the sadness would take over me without warning.

The tears were uncontrollable and difficult to hide. It was a challenge not to break down in front of the children. I'd pretend there was a sad song, or that I had a cold or allergies, and then run to the bathroom. I could not unload or fall apart on them. Not at that time.

A few years later I might be able to tell them how difficult it was for us, as parents. But for now, I had to stay strong for them, so they could be strong. I needed them to believe that we were fine, and that life would be okay. I'm not sure I was able to fool them though–children are emotionally connected to their parents, so they must have felt what I was feeling.

\*\*\*

I wanted David and me to be a strong parenting team for our children, to speak well of each other, focus on the best of each other and support one another. I wanted us to be a strong, healthy divorced family. It was not easy to put this vision into practice. TV shows, movies, gossip magazines and so many other things in our modern culture support "taking him to the cleaners," taking all his money, getting back at "the bitch," and so on. And lawyers didn't inspire us to get along either. After seeing one once to know my rights, I understood right away that making our relationship work was not part of the lawyer's job. Instead, they wanted us to be angry at each other. It's easier to go after the money when one is really mad; that's what they were trained for, to win a case, not save a family. Only later, a few years after the divorce, did I discover a new kind of lawyer—the collaborative lawyer—where the well-being of the family as a whole is their main goal.

As far as family and friends, while they had good intentions, they just didn't know how to help. I needed the support of a legal professional who would understand and respect my goals. Fighting against one another was the exact opposite of what I wanted.

For the most part, David and I were aligned in how we wanted the divorce to happen and how we wanted to raise the children. The financial part was where we needed the most help, where we did not understand each other. During my coaching program, I learned that money is a huge trigger for people, and that was true in our case as well. Money is never about money, but about one's value, fears, power and resentments. Our finances were a major source of fights when we were married, and divorce only made it harder; creating more fears and more resentments.

After researching the various options and who could understand what we were trying to achieve, I decided mediation would be the best route. I found a financial mediator that could work with us, together as a team. Her role was to help us figure out a plan, without taking sides. She had extensive knowledge of the financial, legal and emotional aspects of divorce. She understood that we wanted to work together for the good of the children and to create a happy life after divorce. She helped us manage our emotions, helped us envision the future, and had our best interest at heart.

We saw her five or six times. The first two were mostly to understand what documents we needed to provide, and explain the divorce process. After that, the financial negotiation started, and strong emotions came to the surface. At some point, we were instructed to be in different rooms, as too many angry words were being said. I insisted we agree to never talk about money outside of the mediator's office. It only caused quarrels, and I didn't have it in me to fight anymore. If we started talking about it at home, I removed myself from the conversation, saying, "We agreed we wouldn't talk about it without the mediator."

Society somehow deemed that being a full-time homemaker has no real value in today's currency, and my husband felt the same way. A stay-at-home mom or dad is viewed as monetarily worthless. None of the financial support I gave him while he was in school or to start his company was recognized. In his eyes, I was just a gold digger and a tick, trying to take everything from him, even though everything was split down the middle. No matter what I would get or give, he believed that I took it all. It was extremely painful to see how little my husband thought of my contribution. I felt worthless.

Toward the end of the mediation process, we were instructed to see individual lawyers to review our financial agreement. The comments I heard from my lawyer were: "Well, you can get more here, and there, and there, and there." I could either go back to the mediator to negotiate and fight for more money, or leave it the way it was. I chose to leave it as it was, as my children's and my needs were covered. I knew that "more, more, more" would cost me a whole lot more in the long term. Peace and harmony also have a price. The divorce, up to this point, had taken such a toll on my emotional well-being that I needed to move on as quickly as possible. Ultimately, though, regardless of how the split between David and me happened, he felt I had taken everything from him.

Having a strong and healthy relationship with David was far more important than trying to get more money, yet it was very difficult to see the father of my children hardly acknowledge my part in our family and our finances, over the last sixteen years. I had to learn to detach, and remind myself that it was because he was upset and scared. Still, it was sad to see how little value I had in his eyes.

Once we reached an agreement, we were able to be in the same room again to finish filing all the papers. There was still resentment, sadness, and anger, but with the financials completed, we felt calmer as we gained a glimpse of how we would live our lives. We were no longer in the grey zone, we now could start making plans.

The parenting plan was fairly easy to put together, as we mostly agreed on how we wanted to raise the children. By order of the court, and by choice, we agreed to share the children fifty-fifty. We looked at different plans, and talked to a child therapist to know which one would be the best for the children, and for us. Since the youngest was only five years old, we decided to split the week so they would not go as long as three days before they could see either one of us. We decided with whom the children would spend Christmas eve, Christmas, Thanksgiving, birthdays, Easter, New Year's, Mother's Day, Father's Day, and so on. We also talked about trips to France, as it is very important for the children to still have a relationship with their heritage, and with their family overseas. David always completely agreed with this and never argued against my taking them for longer periods of time. We also discussed how we would parent and agreed that we were still going to make all the decisions together when it came to school, their health, or their upbringing. We changed the parenting plan two years later to a week on, a week off, as the kids got older.

To us, this plan was just a piece of paper that helped us start our divorced life. It never meant that we had to follow it to the letter, and knew we could change it as we saw fit. But it is a necessary document to fall back on, in case something terrible should occur and we could no longer work together. We, as individuals and as a family, grow and change.

The parenting plan and the financial agreement were the first blueprints of our future life as a divorced family. Knowing what you can afford helps you decide where you can live, the type of housing, loans, and the lifestyle choices you can expect. It was a huge stepping-stone and probably the most difficult one. There was such a great relief when that part was completed.

We were ready to go in front of the judge and have her approve our agreements so we could officially be divorced, and tell the children. The appointment was set for September.

# Chapter Nine

## Telling The Children

I knew we couldn't shield our children completely from the pain and fear of our divorce, but I wanted to learn how I could protect them from being badly hurt. While our relationship seemed to get better, it was just a veil. The pain was still very much inside, and many tears were still pouring out of my heart. I did more rescarch on children and divorce and decided to see a child therapist. I wanted guidance from a professional who would understand them, and have their best interest at heart. I wanted my husband to come with me to be on the same page, to hear for himself what the expert had to say, and to ask questions if he had any.

We learned what we would need to say and what not to say, and the importance of not blaming each other or sharing personal details. It would have been easy to go the finger-pointing route, but too damaging to the children. We did not want them to take sides, to be angry at one or the other. We needed them to believe that they had a mom and a dad who loved them, and that we would be their parents, all their lives. We did not rush home to tell our children, we waited as long as we could. Neither of us were prepared in our hearts to have the "Mom and Dad are getting divorced" conversation. I was so afraid of seeing them fall to pieces before our eyes.

We decided to wait to tell them until the divorce became final in September; we didn't want them to go through the fear of the unknown and angst of "What will happen when Mom and Dad get divorced?" Months went by as we waited. School would start in less than a month, and I needed to tell their teachers beforehand what was coming so they could be of support. I no longer had the luxury to wait for the divorce to be final to tell my kids, afraid that they would find out from someone else. Bad news always spread very quickly in a small community. The time had come, we needed to tell them now.

One Sunday morning, as everyone seemed to be in a good mood, I felt in my heart that this was the time to call a family meeting. I remember my husband looking at me with huge panic in his eyes that said,

"What the f---- are you doing?" I looked back at him and said with my eyes, softly, "Trust me, this is the time." Everyone gathered on the bed, wondering what we were going to talk about. And I started.

While we were having this dreaded conversation, there was a sense of togetherness and tenderness. We were holding each other's hands, being a loving, united family. We tried to explain the reasons without going into the details. We told them that we had been arguing too much for too long, and that it kept us from being happy. We explained that Daddy and Mommy had decided it would be better for all of us if he and I lived in different houses so we could be happier. And then... I lied... I spontaneously lied to my kids. I told them that we had divorced a few months ago.

Was it right to lie? I don't know. I just couldn't bear the idea that my children would wake up with panic attacks and anxiety, and I didn't want them to be afraid of the future. So, I lied. I thought that if they believed that we were already divorced, and they did not see big changes in our relationship, it would reassure them that they still had both their parents, and we were still a family who loved each other very much. It was so hard not to fall apart in front of them, but I had to be strong and swallow my tears. We all were heartbroken, but we were heartbroken *together*.

Each child responded differently.

My daughter (then five years old) was happy. She focused on all the positives we were trying to convey. She thought it was going to be "awesome," and was excited to have two houses and happier parents. More one-on-one time with Mom and Dad sounded like heaven to her. It was only after we left the family home, that she realized being in two houses was not as good as she imagined. She wanted to have her parents back in one house so she always could see both of us every day. After three years of divorce, she still wishes that, from time to time, even if she knows that her parents are happier.

My youngest son (then seven years old) was shocked and felt truly heartbroken. He asked a few questions, like, "Where will we live? Where will the cat live?" I could see he was trying to figure out exactly what it would mean to him and our family. Liam has a tendency to spiral into dark thoughts and to get anxious. I could see that's where he was going, so I kept reassuring him that we would always be a family, and that Mom and Dad would always be there for him and for each other. As for the cat, he followed the children.

My nine-year-old son, shut down. When the conversation was finished, without a word, he left the house for a walk. I didn't try to follow him, I knew he needed his alone time. When he came back twenty minutes later, I asked him if he wanted to say anything. All he said was, "This is very sad." I agreed with him, took him in my arms, and we cried together. I held him tight, and we stayed like that for a few minutes. He dried his tears, and went on with his day. Timo has always kept his emotions to himself.

I also told them it was okay to tell their friends if they wanted, and that they were always welcome to come to us. I wanted them to know they could talk to us about anything and that we would always be there for them. I never had any taboo subject with my children, and was not about to start. If they had a question, then they deserved an answer.

While I have always been in tune with my kids and able to guide them, I felt that I needed help to take them through this very difficult time, and decided to take them to see a professional. I did not want to wait until everyone had completely fallen apart to seek help. I talked with a friend who had gone through divorce a few years before, and she recommended an excellent play therapist, Jeremy Dion, out of Lafayette, just a few minutes away. They needed support and a safe place to express their emotions, either by talking or by playing, especially for my oldest son, since he internalized his pain and would not say anything.

I, too, needed this therapist to teach me how to help my kids through our divorce, and the new life we were about to start. It was very important for David and I to go with them. At the beginning of each session, we'd talk with the therapist about what was going on, what we were seeing, then each child had their alone time with him. Then we would re-enter the room. Sometimes the final part was just the parents, and sometimes it included the children. It was teamwork. The therapist would assess the state of mind of the children, help us to support them, and give us tools to communicate and handle the stress. It took about eight sessions for my oldest son, and just two for the other two children.

I also had a couple of sessions with the child therapist on my own. While David and I were committed to a Beautiful Divorce, there were days where I felt we headed straight to "ugly town," with so many painful emotions to work through. No matter how beautiful I wanted our divorce to be, we did step on each other's toes, occasionally. We had to relearn a new dance. We had some letting go to do and some new behaviors to learn. I spent an enormous amount of time monitoring my children's emotions and behaviors, as well as David's, as I was committed to make it work for all of us, for our family. At times, it felt too much—as if I was carrying everyone's emotions, and I had no one to carry mine.

It took so much strength to be the torch holder. I shared my thoughts with my friends and family, but no one truly understood my vision, or knew how to support me. Many of them thought the idea was noble, but could not grasp why I still wanted to have a beautiful relationship with David. Many of them were saying: that's not supposed to happen; if you divorce, then you are not supposed to be friends with your ex-husband. Or some would ask why I would care if David was okay or not. After all, I was getting a divorce. What they did not grasp, is that once we are a family, we are a family forever. The best way I found to describe this concept to them was: We are all in a pool, and if one poops in the pool, we all swim in it.

Of all the people I spoke with, the child therapist was the only person who truly understood what I was building and creating for the five of us. With him, I never had to prove or defend what I was doing; he got it because he recognized the impact it had on the children, and on our family. It would have been so easy to just say, forget it; I am done; I don't want to work at it anymore. I don't care if David and I get along. And there were times I had those thoughts, but I knew that my future, my happiness and the well-being of my children depended on the relationship I was creating with David, as a divorced couple. He gave me the encouragement, the tools and the strength I needed to keep going, and to not give up.

\*\*\*

One afternoon, not long after our "family divorce talk," I got upset with Liam. He was not behaving properly. While it was okay and understandable to act out, there were still some guidelines to respect, and a divorce was not going to end this. I was still raising my children to be good kids and to respect each other. I saw his eyes fill with tears. I could see his pain wasn't because of our silly argument, but was simply a trigger to expose the pain in his heart. I took him tightly in my arms, without a word, and let him cry. He cried in my arms for forty-five minutes while I was caressing his hair and covering him with kisses. His heart was open, and the pain inside was released.

What was the pain about? Do we really know? Or do we hurt and only know we have tears that we must cry? When my mom died, we cried briefly, one time, all together, and then we lived a life of pretense, as if my mother never existed. After her death, there was no one to take us in their arms for us to fully release the pain and to be with our grief. If we cried, we were judged for it. Tears were a sign of weakness, and we had to learn to be strong. So my siblings, father, and I learned to hold in our tears, or to cry quickly, alone in silence behind closed doors. The tears became stuck in my heart, and they are still trying to get out, forty years later. I did not want that for my child. I did not want him to carry that pain for the rest of his life. So I let him cry in my arms, holding him tight and loving him for as long as he needed. He eventually stopped, gave me a big hug and went on with his day. He had nothing to explain. His tears said it all.

# Chapter Ten

## I Now Pronounce You Divorced

Sixteen years earlier, when we got married at the courthouse, the Justice of the Peace said, "I now pronounce you husband and wife. You may kiss the bride." This time, after a few questions to make sure that we both agreed to the terms, all we got was, "You are now divorced." The judge disappeared and there was silence. Nothing, not one word. So, there I was, looking at my newly ex-husband in the courtroom next to me, not knowing what to do.

Now what? Do I kiss him? Do I smile at him? Do I talk to him? What??? Please, somebody tell me. But nothing was said. For a second, I wanted to rewind everything, and run into his arms, and forget it ever happened. We looked at each other, trying to show no emotion, and walked out of the courtroom, next to each other, in silence.

Outside was a beautiful blue sky. Life was exactly the same as when we went in. The birds were still singing, the river was still flowing, the cars were still passing by, and people were still walking around. I suddenly felt small and insignificant, like what happened in my life didn't matter much. I looked at him and said, "I'll see you later at home." We hugged and parted ways. I got into my car, in shock, I suppose. It was too much for my brain.

Yes, the papers said I was divorced, but I didn't feel divorced as I continued to live in our family home until I could find a suitable place for my children and me. Somehow, I thought my life was going to be completely different at that moment. Yet I was the same person, with the same feelings.

My heart was overflowing with emotions: grief, fear, relief, hope, calm, fear, fear, fear, and more sadness; oh, my God. As I was driving home, the tears flowed down my face. It was real; I was no longer married to the man I had loved so much, for so long. I couldn't think of the hurt we both endured during our marriage anymore but only the good moments that we shared. Now what? Who was I supposed to be? What was I supposed to do? I had no answer.

In hindsight with regard to all divorced families, I wish the judge had said, "I now pronounce you divorced. You are bonded by your children for life. You are responsible for their happiness, so make sure you work together. You are no longer husband and wife, but you are still mother and father. Never forget that. You may now go home, kiss your children, and be good parents."

# Chapter Eleven

## Had I become highly contagious?

**I** could not have predicted my friends' reaction to my divorce or how judgmental some were. Many removed themselves from my life, when I needed them the most; they ran away, and it hurt like hell. They were afraid of the pain, the drama, and that it could happen to them.

I recall having lunch at a friend's house, who regularly invited us for dinners with her family. But that day, I could feel something was off, so I asked her what was going on. With hesitation first, she finally said that three kids and me were a bit much. It was like a punch to the stomach. How could my kids and me be too much, but not too much when David was with us? I looked at her, trying to keep it together, called my children and left. Other friends stopped inviting me over because I didn't have a significant other, assuming it would make things uncomfortable at dinner parties. Women became afraid that I would hit on their husbands, and their husbands were afraid that somehow I would convince their wives to get a divorce. Family dinner invitations lessened, replaced by one-on-one coffee dates. Some didn't understand why I would do a stupid thing like getting a divorce, and immediately stopped talking to me. Some thought I didn't fit the perfect family image anymore; my existence threatened their ideal. Some thought I shouldn't be having a relationship with my ex. They removed me from their life because it didn't make any sense to them. And for some, I was a constant reminder of the divorce they might have been thinking about for years, but were too scared to face their fears of truth.

People stay away when they don't understand you, and few like to question their beliefs. I learned to accept all these things, but that didn't make it less painful. I wasn't contagious, and I was not about to steal their husbands, or try to convince anyone to divorce. All I wanted was to still have my friendly community.

As for the ones who stayed, although many said they thought the concept of Beautiful Divorce was great, they did not know how to help or support us. I just needed their compassion and trust. Instead, I was constantly explaining the how's and why's. It was exhausting.

People were compelled to take sides right away, and started bashing David. I had to nip that in the bud. I could not allow others to badmouth my children's father. My divorce was based on respect, caring and kindness. Some people even called him an "asshole," without really knowing him, assuming this was what I wanted to hear. I had to ask friends, family and strangers to show him respect. I committed to act towards him the way I wanted him to treat me. And I certainly did not want my children to hear anything bad about their daddy. That would have hurt them too much.

Bit by bit, I made new friends, mostly women who were single mothers and divorced. Since we finally had some time off from being a full-time mom, together we made the best of it. During that first year, they helped me enjoy life again. We supported each other, we became like a family: going out together, listening to music, dancing, taking short trips, nurturing each other when we felt sick, talking about the pain and the challenges of divorce. I am so grateful to have had those women in my life during that time. It would have been very easy to stay at home and feel sorry for myself. Instead, we pushed each other out of our funk and encouraged each other to live life to its fullest.

What I now realize is that losing friends during that period was actually a good thing. They did not have the tools to support me in what I was going through, so they stepped aside to make room for the ones who did. After a few years, some of them came back, reassured that I was not going to suck them into my drama or put them in a difficult situation. A few invited me and David and his new girlfriend to the same parties. They don't necessarily understand our relationship, but they respect it and are not afraid of it. I've even had a few people come to me and say, if I ever get divorced, I want to do it your way.

# Chapter Twelve

## My New Home

**I** started looking for a new place as soon as the financial agreement was signed. I found a place that would be perfect for the children and me. It was just a few blocks away from David, so the children could still walk back and forth between the two houses, see their neighborhood friends, and walk to school just like they did before the divorce.

The new place needed some work done to be fully livable, so David and I agreed that I would stay in the family home until the house was ready for us to move in a few months later.

Very little had changed in our lives. We were still the same people, living almost the same way as before the divorce. We still had family dinners every night, did family gatherings with the five of us, and even took a trip to Africa to visit David's brother. His family and friends were uncomfortable with me going, but we were fine. They could not understand what we were doing, or why in the world we would want to spend time together now that we had divorced. We had become kinder to each other and already happier. We still triggered each other with familiar arguments as before, but less often and with less intensity. Life overall seemed better.

Early February 2014, my new house was finally ready. Renovations always take longer than expected, and as with all old houses, my contractor kept finding things that had to be fixed. Moving to my new home was very exciting. I was completely free to decorate it the way I wanted, to choose all the colors, to listen to music I wanted... or to be in complete silence. I rediscovered the joy of dancing in the middle of the kitchen and walking naked if I wanted to.

But when the children moved in a few days later, nothing was like I imagined. I was looking for excitement and joy, but our first night was anything but joyful. It felt awkward, as if we had no idea how to move around, like strangers in someone else's house. It felt like a nice house but not home. The children hated it, and couldn't wait to go back to their father's. They wanted to sleep in their bed, watch TV on their couch, the way it used to be. It's really at that moment that we all felt the consequences of our divorce. While I loved this house and saw the future in it, I too felt like a stranger. It wasn't our home.

Eventually, we all made our marks and found our places. They started to like the house and I loved it. Now, a few years after the divorce, the children feel completely at home when they come. They like the differences between the two houses. In one, they have space, as their dad has a much bigger house, and in mine they feel the closeness. We have three bedrooms (the boys still share one) and the main room that includes the kitchen and the living room. While I cook dinner, the kids do their homework or play around. We have conversations, and everyone is part of it. I have made them part of my team as well. While I am still the parent, they see that I cannot do everything alone. They help me with dinner, with clean up, and by helping each other with their homework. Everyone has a job and a part in this family. We are all in it, and we have found our rhythm.

# Chapter Thirteen

## Being The Strength For My Babies

**A** few weeks after moving in, I was by myself outside shoveling snow, while the children were at their daddy's. There was silence and there was sunshine. Things were looking up and I was adapting to my single life, when the panic struck. How was I going to pull it off? How was I going to take care of a house, the back and front yard, the garage, the car, the kitchen, the cleaning, the making of money... and the children, their emotions—and me and my emotions? The reality was overwhelming. It seemed so much for just one person. I was filled with doubts and needed someone to tell me I'd be okay, that I'd find a way to make it work.

My dad had been alone when he raised four kids. He seemed so solid, like he had it together. He was my rock, my safety net, and my role model. He always seemed to know what to do, or what to say to reassure me. After his death, David became my rock and my person to go to when my heart was aching. He became my security.

My dad was now dead, and I had just divorced my rock. I felt alone and little, like a four-year-old in a world of grown-ups. I started talking to my dad, hoping that maybe his soul or his voice in my heart would tell me something. "How did you do it, Daddy? How were you so strong? How were you able to do all that, all by yourself? I so need you right now; please tell me what to do, tell me how to do it?" Suddenly this came to me: "YOU are now THEIR rock. Be strong for THEM."

Of course! My children! They have always been my source of courage. They give me the strength to get back up and keep moving. I am no longer my father's child; I am now the mother of my children. I am *their* safety net, *their* security, *their* rock.

Realizing this gave me new strength and suddenly my fears disappeared. While most of my days are quite happy, I still have some days that I feel down, but I keep going for them. I want them to be happy, to be good people, and to embrace life. I must teach them how to do that by example.

\*\*\*

From the moment they were born, my children came first. They became my reason for living, my passion, my drive, my love. Nothing and no one mattered more than my children.

I learned how to parent from my father. As a widower, he was the only one who raised us; there was no parenting team. He did what he thought was best for us kids, without discussing it with anyone. I now realize that when I was married, I parented as if I were the only parent. I was making the decisions regarding my children and my husband went along with it. Now that David and I were divorced, and that he was parenting half the time, I needed to learn to become part of a team and parent together.

I was working full-time when my first child was born. After that, I worked less and less, and three kids later, I was a full-time, stay-at-home mom. I took care of their health, nutrition, education, development, and their happiness. I stayed up all night when they were sick, cooked every meal, went to every school event, volunteered in their classrooms, helped with homework, took them to activities, and arranged playdates. I listened to them, counseled them, and was there for them one hundred percent. They came before anything or anyone, including my husband and me.

Our children are the next generation. They will be the ones who someday run our country, the decisions makers, business owners, doctors, nurses, teachers, scientists, politicians; it is up to us, as parents, to prepare them to become the kind of person we want to fill those roles. I take my job very seriously. My love for my children has given me the courage to do new things and step out of my comfort zone. They make me look at myself as no one has done; they make me question if I am a good person, how can I change, how I can be kinder, how to give my best: A life to be proud of. If I expect that of my kids, then I have to demand that of myself.

The day I had to let go of my kids fifty percent of the time was not easy. Although I knew I would enjoy some me time, which I rarely allowed myself before, it was hard to process. I would not be the only main caretaker anymore, and it scared me to death. At the time, I thought I knew better than anyone how they should be raised.

I had to learn to let them go. I had to trust that their dad was going to do the best he could, and that he was going to be great at it. How could I support him to be a good daddy for our children? How would he remember all the playdates and activities, what to have them wear, what to bring to school, and when to do homework. Could he actually prepare dinner, and at the same time have them read, and ready for bed by 8:00 pm? How would he know our daughter liked to have her ear pulled when falling asleep, or to gently stroke my son's back when he was upset? And how would he know how to soothe them when they were sick? I had never let him do it on his own for more than a few days. How were they going to survive? My babies...

I had been a mom for the last ten years, and it took me all that time to learn to be a great mom. I had to trust that their dad could do that too. I wanted him to succeed in being a good dad for my kids, and I wanted my kids to be happy with him, even without me there.

I knew he would make mistakes right from the beginning, after all, it took me years to be the mom I am today. I had to be as helpful and supportive as I could for him to learn. Instead of nagging him about doing things wrong, as I did in our marriage, I decided to focus on what he did right and encourage him to do more.

So I learned to shut up. When I saw my ex-husband do something "wrong," I shut up. When he forgot to take the kids to their activities, I shut up. Awful lunches? same. (Although I did say something after a whole year of ham sandwiches.) Anytime the kids said nice things about their dad, and their time with him, I'd tell him and thank him. I stopped nagging, and started acknowledging him for all the good things he was doing and being. If I thought he might forget an event, I would gently remind him by saying, "Hey, do you need help to get a present for the party on Saturday?" instead of, "Don't forget about the party Saturday."

Eventually, he and the children created their own space, their own way and their new life together. He'll never cook like me, he'll never cuddle them like I do, but his ways are sometimes better than mine. I have always admired how David lives life to the fullest. He works smart; he makes time for biking, for swimming, and to have fun with friends. He has the perfect work-life balance, and he teaches the children how to achieve that too.

I had to learn to trust that he could parent as well as I could. I wish I had done that much earlier, but I can't go back... only do better in the future.

We support each other enormously in our quest to be better parents. Where I used to do so much alone, we now go together to the parent-teacher conferences, to the dentist and to the doctor. And if there are times when he can't join me, I let him know everything that's been said or done. If he has to miss a school event where the kids perform, I take pictures and videos to share with him, so he is not missing out. I still call him to talk about the kids if something is not working, or if I have worries. If I observe attitude or grades going down, or anything unusual, I call him to discuss. Just a few weeks ago, one of my boys was acting up, so I asked David to step in and talk with him. He called our son and instructed him to respect and listen to me. It is very important for my children to know that their mom and dad will always work together to make decisions about raising them. Sure, they tried to play us at the beginning of the divorce. If daddy says no to something, maybe mommy will say yes. Well, they tried only once and got an earful! They understood that we were a tight parenting team and always discussing them.

# Chapter Fourteen

## Communicating With the Person Who Broke Your Heart

Now that we were divorced, communication had to change as well. We no longer could talk to each other the way we did in our marriage. There were new rules and new boundaries. I was not his wife anymore, but we were still parents and had to connect regularly. Most divorced people I know either don't talk to each other or they do it in conflict. I did not want to feel anger or hate every time I had to see him. What would that teach our children? What kind of life would that create for them and for me? I didn't want them to learn how to hate; I wanted them to learn that it was possible to still love and respect one another, even with fundamental differences.

So, I thought about how we communicate with our colleagues, our bosses and friends, and realized I would never lash out at them the way I did with my spouse. Imagine going to work, and because you had a bad day, you start yelling at your colleague. That might get you fired. David was now my partner in parenting. Lashing out at him was no longer an option, and would only bring strife to the family.

We had to learn to treat each other more like business partners—the business being our family. That was my model as I reconfigured our relationship. I listened more, we talked about the kids, not so much about him or about me. I learned to speak with more clarity and more kindness. We talked about ourselves when we needed support from each other.

We practiced respecting each other's boundaries and limits, learning what we should or should not discuss. Sometimes, the topics were complicated, such as how to handle a new mate in the mix. How would David's new partner affect me, or the children? And would it change the way my kids relate to me? I had to separate my emotions from the emotions of the children. Once I was clear on this, I would talk with him.

Of course, we had a few hurdles. We were both learning a new dance, and it was natural that we would step on each other's toes. While it was a difficult transition, it also taught me to pick my battles and choose when to stand strong, and when to let go.

To be clear, my beautiful divorce was not about agreeing to everything so no one gets upset. It was about finding out who I was, what I was committed to, what was most important to my family and me. It taught me to stand up for what I believed in, in a way I never was able to do before.

In the long run, we both have become better parents and better people. We communicate and move through conflict with more respect and compassion.

# Chapter Fifteen

## Facing My Emotions

Overall, my life was in a positive place. I had a good relationship with David, the children were doing well, I loved my new home, and I had great new friends.

I had spent the last two years holding everything and everyone together, constantly explaining and reminding, guiding, coaching, and keeping them on track, in order to rebuild the infrastructure of our family. Everyone seemed to know now where his or her place was in this new life. The family foundation was strong and stable.

I could finally breathe and let my emotions come to surface. I had repressed all the negative ones of my failed marriage and my divorce so, I could build the life I wanted to live. It was time to look inside to see what I needed to deal with. Sadly, anger was the first to pop up. I could feel it rise and poison my heart. It got to a point where I couldn't contain it anymore; it was taking me over. I was angry for everything, all the time, and I could not understand why. My life was going well, I was achieving what I wanted. But I stopped feeling gratitude and had descended into the dark side of the moon. Everything seemed difficult or demanded a fight.

Was I angry because David had found someone else so quickly, and I had not? Was I angry for all the things that went wrong in my marriage? I am not sure, but I knew it had to stop. It was hurting me, and more importantly, my kids. I would snap at them on a whim, and I sure did not like that. Here I was saying that I would do anything for them, I would even die for them, and there I was, hurting their hearts.

I talked to spiritualists, therapists, life coaches, and friends. All had something to say about letting go anger, but none of their input changed a thing, until I met this lady who understood me, and saw me differently. She suggested that I expressed myself through art. Painting is like meditation for me; I can spend hours on a canvas thinking of nothing, painting my guts out. She asked me to paint my anger. I drew a dragon spewing flames at a child. Tears were pouring down the child's face. At that moment, like a mirror, I truly saw for the first time who I was when I was upset, and how it hurt my children. My heart was broken, and the reasons for my anger did not matter anymore. I had to stop lashing out at them. I had to find another way.

I learned to fight the fire inside and breathe it out. I would tell my kids when the anger was rising, and excuse myself for a "time out" before saying things I might regret. Slowly, the fire was contained. I focused on the good things, and what I wanted for the future. I noticed everything my ex was doing right. I looked for the positive. I focused on the moment and being happy. It wasn't easy when the fire was in my belly. Another way that seems to work very well for me is intense workout. A few years later, the anger came back. I could feel the fire inside, and once again, had no clue why. I started boxing, and it did the trick. Not only did it tame the dragon, but it was making me breath, and that's what I truly needed at the time. Deep breaths.

I also told my children that it was okay to tell me if I was being hurtful. Timo, my oldest son, is usually the one to stand up and tell me if I am doing something wrong. It's not pleasant to hear, but it pulls me out of myself. I am not always the wonderful mother I wish I could be, and sometimes need a reality check to be that person. I have enlisted my kids to help me be a better mother. It is sometimes very difficult to hear what your children have to say about you, but they often tell the truth. There is no more effective way of becoming a better person than to listen to the honest feedback of those who love you.

# Chapter Sixteen

## Finding Gratitude

David and I agreed on paper that I would have the children for my birthday. However, as the day approached, I thought it would be nice to have some time to celebrate with friends as well, so we agreed that I would see the children for a few hours, and have the rest of the day free. A few weeks before my birthday, my head started playing games, trying to make me feel lonely, and alone; that I was not going to receive presents, that I suck and I'm unworthy. I didn't want to go down that sad road, so I reached out to friends and made plans to not be alone that day.

I woke up on the morning of my birthday, waiting for the sadness to hit me. My kids were still sleeping. It was a beautiful day. I got up and consciously decided I was going to have a good day. I started breakfast, the kids got up, and then came the hugs, kisses, and happy birthday wishes. After a yummy breakfast, I took the kids to their daddy. To my greatest surprise, my ex-husband had a present for me. It was a candle. I had tears of joy sliding down my cheeks. I truly thought I wasn't going to receive any presents, especially not from him. For the first time, I truly understood the word gratitude, and it filled my heart. I felt worthy, appreciated, and cared for. He was being nice to the mother of his children, and I will always respect and recognize him for that. After dropping off the children, I went back home to find a beautiful bouquet of flowers and a card from a friend, in front of my door. How wrong was I to believe that no one would remember or care about my birthday?

Later that evening, a few girlfriends came over to step out and play. They organized a day on the water, paddle boarding, with drinks and cake. I was surrounded by love, and happiness followed, as if life was reminding me that I was not alone. That birthday was a stepping-stone. I learned that I am never alone if I choose not to be, and that a gift is not just a present, but a reminder that someone is trying to make me happy.

# Chapter Seventeen

# My Ex-Husband's First New Girlfriend

Just a few months after I moved out of the marital house, I found out that David had started dating and had already fallen in love with another woman. I was surprised at how fast he met someone, and how quickly they became serious. While we had agreed to trust each other to pick the right time to introduce new significant others to the children, I felt like he had let this woman into their lives too fast.

While I was concerned about my children, my own heart surprised me. I was not prepared for him to be with someone else so soon. Maybe it shouldn't have mattered since I divorced him, but it did. It was difficult to see myself being replaced so quickly. It was painful to watch him share his life and laughs with someone else, as we were still sharing and talking almost every day. I knew that at some point, it would lessen, but not just so soon. The day I heard he had a sleepover, I sensed something was up. David was not the kind of person to have casual sex. If he spent a night with a woman, he was giving his heart to her.

I was curious and I wanted to know everything about her. After work, I stopped by his house. I needed to know the raw truth. I needed to face the reality that he was moving on, so I too, could move on, even if it hurt like hell. I bombarded him with questions and asked him to be as honest and sincere as possible. He asked me if I really wanted to know, feeling a bit uncomfortable, but let it all out.

I felt surges of sadness, jealousy, and happiness while he described his new love. Tears flowed out of me. I was happy he'd found someone, but insecurity struck, and I started asking him comparative questions. Is she taller than me; is she prettier than me; is she funnier than me? Right then, he said: "Sandrine, please stop. She is not like you; no one is like you. You will never be replaced. You are unique. I just want to try something different."

His words immediately calmed my insecurity. He was right; no one will ever be like me. No one could erase our sixteen years of marriage. She would not replace me as the mother of our three children. It was the best gift he could have given me. That one sentence changed my life. It planted a deep strength and confidence in my heart. No one will ever replace me. Yes, I'm no longer his wife, his lover, his confidante, but I will forever be the mother of his children.

I no longer had the fear that I could be replaced. I found my place, which is in my own heart and in my family's heart. For the first time in my life I felt rooted, like a 150 year-old oak tree: strong and solid. I will always love my children, and they will always love me. Adding someone else in the family mix wouldn't change any of that. In fact, if it added happiness to their lives, it would bring happiness to mine. Happy daddy, happy children, happy mommy.

If David loved her, she must be quite an amazing woman. So, I created an image in my head, a vision where my family would grow to six people, only adding more love in the mix. Much easier said than done.

While I was happy for him, I also felt hurt. Even as I became stronger and more confident, I was jealous as I read posts about their love story on Facebook. I couldn't shake the feeling that it was supposed to be me in those pictures; it was supposed to be me taking those wonderful trips with him. They were living the dream I had when I married him, but now, another woman was living it. I didn't want to be jealous, and I wanted them to feel free to love each other. After all, I was the one who asked for the divorce. What right did I have to be jealous? Yet this was how I felt at the moment, and to heal, I needed to protect my heart and allow them to share their love, without fear of hurting me. I "unfriended" him, his family and friends on Facebook. I could not bear to see the comments about how happy people were for them.

Questions and anxiety started to fill my head once more: What would it mean to my children and our family? Would they love her more than me? At that moment, I made myself believe that the love of my children was not going to change just because someone else loved them, or because they loved one more person. My love for my first child didn't change when I had my second child; I just had more in my heart. My strongest drive has always been for the happiness of my children. If I had to put my feelings, insecurities, and fears aside so my children could be happy, then so be it; I would.

.

After a couple of months of David and this new woman dating, she and I felt it was time for us to meet. She'd already met my children and was spending more and more time with them. The kids seem to like her, and I wanted to know her and like her too. We decided to meet at my ex-husband's house. On the way there, my heart was pounding hard, so I stopped a few times to breathe and re-center myself. She was in the front yard playing ball with my children. I came toward them with a big smile and hugged them all. She was indeed very different than me physically. I am petite dark blond, and she was a towering, long dark-haired woman. After greeting each other, we decided to go for a bike ride, just the two of us. It seemed easier to talk than sitting across a table interrogating each other, with David around. We spent a couple of hours discussing our roles and expectations.

She was intelligent, kind, funny, and crazy in love with my ex-husband, and my children. In return, they were all crazy about her. I put my feelings of jealousy aside and welcomed her into our family with open arms. She loved the idea of our partnership in parenting and wanted to be encouraging and supportive. The two of us met a few times over the next months, and had wonderful conversations. We both needed to figure out how to be in this new relationship. We talked about boundaries, and shared our fears and dreams. Everything seemed to be working out. Then, doubt, fear, jealousy and insecurity got to her, and things started going awry.

She and David began fighting more. It seemed that I was usually the topic of their fights, which, in turn, created tension between David and me. Although his girlfriend tried, she was not able to handle our tight parenting relationship. She did not understand why we communicated so often. She asked him to take down all the family photos, and anything that could remind her of me. She didn't understand why we wanted to be all together for Christmas and birthdays. She didn't understand why I was still so present in their lives.

When She and I talked about those feelings, it seemed to appease her fears. I wanted her to be an ally and not have us fear each other. But to make things worse, her therapist (an ex- nun who never was married or had children) asked why should David and I wait months or years to wean from each other? We should just pull away quickly, like pulling off a bandage. We should not have a relationship anymore, and I should not be in the picture.

All that might have been fine if we did not have young children. She couldn't bare that I would always be in their lives, sharing all the special moments; the first day of school, their birthdays, teacher conferences, graduations, doctors, the day my children would have children, and every other occasion that would be about our children.

David and I were attached by our children for the rest of our lives. She could not handle that. She told me that sharing the people she loved the most was too much for her. She tried to manage her feelings of jealousy and insecurity, but they always seemed to overpower her heart and stop her from seeing how good our situation was. She couldn't get beyond her belief that I wanted David back, as there was no hate between David and me, but rather, complicity and kindness for each other.

Her fears created tension with David, with him and me, and with her and me. We tried to be together for events with the children, but the feeling was oppressive. She watched us like a hawk. If he smiled at me or I laughed with him, she would get upset. Getting together became stressful and unpleasant. Yet I was not going to remove myself from my kids' life because she could not manage me being there.

The first family holiday with her was *Thanksgiving*. We had agreed in the parenting plan that he would have the children for that time, as this was not part of French culture, and it meant more to him than to me. But, once divorced, to my surprise, this holiday became very important to me as well. I needed to see my kids on that day. I asked David if it would be possible to give them a quick hug, and if not possible, then to have some screen time to see them for a few minutes. David told me that they would all be away in the mountains to celebrate.

The night before Thanksgiving, my phone rang. It was his girlfriend. She screamed in my ear, "It's all your fault. I hope you are happy. We are breaking up and it's all your fault; you can have your family back."

After calming her down for over an hour and guiding her back to him, they were reconciled. Or so I thought. In the morning, as I got ready to leave to celebrate Thanksgiving with my friends, I got a text from her saying, "Thank you for your help, but it did not work. We are coming home. You can be with your kids."

I was baffled. I texted her and David back, trying to understand what was going on, but got no answer. Twenty minutes later, I saw my ten-year-old coming to my house crying, looking at me and shouting, "What did you do?"

I had no idea what was happening, but I was furious. How could my kid blame me? All he knew was that my name kept coming up while his dad and his girlfriend were fighting. After many calls and texts, David finally got back to me. Everything was under control, he said. The kids still would have Thanksgiving at home with him and his girlfriend. I was shaken and enraged that she hijacked my kids' Thanksgiving the way she did. I left to celebrate with my friends, still worrying and wondering what just happened, and how we'd move on.

Christmas was right around the corner and I knew that it would be a challenge. Before David's girlfriend turned unpleasant, I imagined us all spending it together; but obviously, it was not an option anymore. In the parenting plan, it was written that I would get them for Christmas Eve, and David would get them Christmas Day. I found it sad that my children would not be able to open presents with both their parents. It was another family holiday, and they wanted all of us.

But how could we make it happen without creating more conflict with his girlfriend? This was our first Christmas not together as a family. Juggling which presents to give the kids from dad, from mom, from Santa and the grandparents, seemed a lot of handle.

I wanted to spend Christmas Eve at my place, then bring the kids to their dad and have Santa there in the morning. We'd always had Christmas there, and I wanted to keep some stability for the children. David seemed okay with that plan, but not his girlfriend. She had to work until the afternoon, and the thought that I would spend Christmas morning in David's house without her, was too much. She had been preparing Christmas with him and the kids, decorating and putting presents under the tree. She felt that I would be stealing Christmas from her. I thought it was nonsense.

As I entered David's house, a few weeks before Christmas, I saw the tree with dozens of presents underneath. It looked beautiful and enchanting, just like when we were married, but this time, I was not part of it. All the presents were from her to my children, from David to her, and her to David. It was painful to see that I was not part of it, but had to accept it. I went home to cry and feel sorry for myself.

I called Hans, my coach for support, and he told me: "You can either cry about it, or you can create your own Christmas for you and your kids." He was right. I was crying for what I did not have, instead of focusing on creating what I wanted. I decorated the house with a beautiful tree and garlands everywhere. It was warm and joyful. I could feel the spirit of Christmas embracing me, and the joy came back to my heart. I knew, though, that I still wanted to share Christmas morning with David, so the children had family time with both their parents. I talked with David, and we agreed that he would come to my place. We'd have breakfast, open the presents from Santa, from me, from their dad, and from us as the parental unit. I wanted them to be reassured that we were still a family. David's girlfriend felt heard, and I still got what

I wanted for my children. David came, we opened the presents, and a couple of hours later, he and the kids had another Christmas with his girlfriend, at his place. The children seemed to adapt quite nicely to the divorce, and with David having someone else in his life. They liked her, and she was good to them. But a few months after Christmas, I felt that something was not right. I know when my kids are sick, before any doctor. I know if they are happy or sad before they say a word. I could tell that something was off, really off, especially with Liam, my middle child. I could not explain clearly what was going on, but a shift in their mood or attitude was enough to raise my antennae.

I called David and asked him if anything unusual was happening in their home. He sensed it, too, and told me that Liam had awaken at night a couple of times crying, uncontrollably. While Liam had the most obvious reaction, I sensed something with my other two other children, as well. I asked them if anything was wrong or different at school, with their friends, or at Daddy's. The answer was always no. Yet, I knew something was up, and I had to find out before they completely fell apart.

I took Liam back to see the child therapist to help me figure out what was causing him stress and night anxiety. After the session, the therapist agreed that something was off, but was not able to pinpoint the issue. Children that age don't always have the words to explain how they feel, and Liam could not articulate his pain or his fear.

One evening, a few days after the therapist, I reminded Liam that I was going to pick him up from school the next day since David was away on business. He said I didn't need to do that, as David's girlfriend had already made plans with him. What he did not know, though, is that they just had broken up, and that she was not going to pick him up. She forgot (intentionally or not, I don't know) to inform him. And suddenly it struck me, I finally understood what was going on.

David and his girlfriend had broken up a number of times, leaving the children wondering, unconsciously, if she would be there for them. They had fallen in love with her and believed that she was going to be part of their lives. But again and again, with each breakup, my kids were left not knowing what would happen, which created anxiety. Their lives at their Daddy's had become unstable. I emailed the child therapist and explained to him what I thought. He agreed with my finding, saying that this type of situation could indeed create great stress, and affect their wellbeing. I had to protect them, so I decided to have a heart-to-heart with David.

Communicating with him during this relationship had become very difficult. Her jealousy and insecurity had taken its toll on us, as every time we needed to get in touch (either face to face, emails or text), it resulted in an argument between them, and consequently between us.

He needed to know, from me, that his new love was hurting our children, so I wrote him a letter. I had to be extremely careful with how I was going to write it. After all, he had the right to tell me to butt out. I did not have a say-so in his personal life anymore. I shared my findings at the therapist's. I told him that his relationship with her had to change, or ours as a family. A few days later, after a few email exchanges between David, his girl, and me (as I had been requested to always keep her in the loop when contacting him), David and I received a final breakup letter from her.

Her last words were: "You either need to run back in each other's arms or learn to be divorced."

I guess she meant that we should have the typical divorce where the parents don't communicate, or perhaps hate or dislike each other. In the past eight months, when she would break down, I would come to her rescue, explain to her again that it was not about David and me but our family, that my children loved her and that David loved her. I coached her through the pain to get them back together. This time, though, I was done. I did not want to help anymore. It was too much work and too much pain for all of us.

When they broke up for the last time, I felt a thousand pounds off my shoulders. I had my family back, and the tension melted away. But my heart broke when my daughter said to me, "She left us." It made me realize how children process breakups. It was no longer just about their dad and his girlfriend; it was a breakup for them as well, just like another divorce, and they were caught in the middle. My father never entered another relationship after my mother's death, so I hadn't fully anticipated how David's splitting would impact our children. But very quickly, peace and harmony came back into our lives. Our family was strong, and it taught the children that no matter what happens, mom and dad will always be there for them, as a tight family.

About two months later, I received an email from David's ex-girlfriend, apologizing for the way she behaved. She said that she truly loved my kids, and asked if she could stay in touch with them. We talked on the phone for a few hours to review the whole fiasco. She also said that David had emailed her, repeatedly, begging her to come back, for three weeks. I was stunned. How could he do that when he saw how their relationship was hurting our family? My heart was hurt too. After sixteen years of marriage, all I got from him after I asked for a divorce, was a 3am talk, when he came back from an evening with friends, after too much to drink. I was sleeping, and I did not even understand what he was saying. Did he say he loved me? I am not even sure. So, finding out that he begged her for three weeks to come back to him after having dated her for only eight months was very hurtful. After a year of carrying the guilt of divorce, I realized that he probably wanted this divorce as much as I did; he just didn't have the consciousness or courage to face that harsh reality.

As far as her seeing my kids again, I talked with David about it, and we both decided that it was not a good idea.

# Chapter Eighteen

## My Ex-Husband's New Life Partner

Life was good again. The pressure of David's ex-girlfriend was gone, and our relationship returned to being kind, present and respectful. But about a month after the breakup, as I was talking to my son, he told me that his dad had a new girlfriend. How could he go into a relationship so quickly, especially after what happened? My heart pounded, and I felt very stressed. I went to see David the next day. He was indeed dating again. I got scared and anxious, afraid of a repeat episode of the "last girlfriend." I did not have the strength in me. I just wanted peace and calm, and a new girlfriend was jeopardizing this. I was worried for my children too. What about them? How could they go through that again? I felt that thousand pounds back on my shoulders. I was waiting apprehensively for the train to hit me again... but nothing happened.

My relationship with David was good, no one telling us how to be, how to communicate, if we could see each other, or how to run our family. Not one peep. I started to believe his new relationship might be different.

David was happy, the kids were happy. This time, I didn't want to know much about her, and did not feel the need to talk boundaries. She gave us the space we needed. And she never interfered with my family affairs. I assume she felt similarly because she never reached out to me either. My children had met her and were excited about her. All that was coming back to my ears were good things. So, I let them be.

About six months later, I finally met her, by accident. Her name is Meg. I was at David's to drop off something for the kids. I stayed a little while, shooting the breeze as a friend of ours from Atlanta was there too. I could feel that David was a bit anxious and asked him what was going on. He said that it was work, but then she appeared, and I understood his restlessness. I looked at her with a big smile, hugged her and kissed her on the cheek. I just wanted to thank her for being so accommodating and for making our lives better. She was secure, and not at all threatened by my relationship with David. She had an easy smile, and seemed to be the perfect match for my ex-husband. I could feel that she would be good for us all, trusting that this time, it was going to work. I stayed a few more minutes and left the house with a smile on my face. We were good.

Meg is divorced and has two children of her own. She, too, has a good relationship with her ex-husband, and believes in family. I didn't have to explain or convince her of what we were trying to do. She understood that I was the mother of my children and that David and I raised them as a team. She's always been supportive of our relationship, and very respectful of me.

About a year later, in spring 2016, as I was once again stopping by David's, the children ran toward me and said: "Guess what, guess what? Daddy, can we tell Mommy?" My heart raced, I did not like surprises anymore. And they said: "We are going to move into a new home with Meg." I wasn't prepared for that news, but I tried to be happy for them, even though my heart was crumbling. I knew this day was coming eventually, as David told me they intended to move together in a year or two... but not today! The children went online to show me pictures of the house; it was big and beautiful. But it was not in our neighborhood, and the children would not be able to walk back and forth from our two houses anymore.

I could feel the sadness coming up, and I excused myself. I went outside and David followed. He hugged

147

me tight, and I let the tears out. I told David that I was very happy for them, but there was a lot coming up into my heart that I needed to sort out. The family house was the last tangible link of our marriage, our life together, and I had to let all those memories go. I knew those were my emotions to manage, and with the support of friends, and many tears to cry, I was able to say goodbye. I thought that with the divorce, I would not feel any sadness about our past anymore, but I was wrong. It was still painful to see our chapter be completely over, and the page turning, even though I knew it was inevitable.

After my own emotions, a wave of questions came up: How would Sienna get to school in the morning? The boys were now in another school, biking distance from the new house. How will we still be in touch, as they would no longer be able to 'just drop by" to say hello (which they did daily)? Who would be driving when the kids forget things at one of the houses? And mostly, how was it going to affect my relationship with my kids? Having a girlfriend that visits from time to time is one thing; living with her is another. It was going to be her home, her rules, her ways.

While the kids were excited in the beginning, they began to realize what moving meant to them. Even though, the house was only two miles away (we were currently just four minutes' walk from each other), it would change their daily routines. I listened as they shared their fears. My oldest son cried while telling me how stupid this new house was. Even though it's a gorgeous home in a great neighborhood, across from a beautiful park. My daughter was scared that she would no longer be able to see her friends. For weeks, she kept asking me if we could stop by the new place, and set it on fire so they would stay in the family home. My other son was fine, he loved the idea of having his own room. After weeks of tears and complaints, I went to the child therapist again to learn how I could support them through this transition.

This time I wanted to see him alone, no kids. I too had worries and anger to let out, and needed someone to help me process those emotions. I understood that they loved each other so much that they wanted to live together, but I felt that their decision was only theirs and did not include all the people who were affected. After all, it was no longer about the two of them; their decision to move would impact the lives of my children, her children, and the exes. Of course, I did not have any say, nor did I expect any. However, I would've liked to know their intention before they bought it. I wished I'd been prepared, and had prepared my children for it. Such is life, so we all had to deal with it, on the spot.

The therapist helped me realize that I did not have to shoulder everyone's burden, and did not have to resolve all my children's issues. All I had to do was to offer a safe space for them to express their emotions. That I could do. It gave them an outlet to express themselves, to let go of the tears, and to feel heard and respected.

I was also told to ask my children if they wanted me to share their feelings with their dad. My son said no, but my daughter asked me to talk to him. She was afraid of hurting his feelings. She did not want to move to their new home, and even asked if she could move in with me, permanently. I knew she still wanted to stay with her daddy, and that was just her way to express her fear of change. After a month of tears and complaints, it was time to move forward. I assured her that it was okay to feel those emotions, and she had the right to believe that it sucked, but the reality was that they were moving. I asked what we could do to make that move more pleasant.

So we talked about her room and how she would decorate it to make it her home. She told me that "home" was the family home where she grew up, and that my house and the new house would just be houses, because she had lost her home. It was difficult to hear this. I had worked so hard to make my new house home for them, but it seems that once you get two houses, home is no longer home; there is only Mom's house or Dad's house. She asked me if I intended to move out soon. Both of my boys asked me the same question. They needed to know that their life was not going to completely change anytime soon, and that they needed stability. I too needed it; we all did. And to make this happen, we had to accept that life was about to change, once again, and resisting it would bring more pain. We needed to create a new routine for everyone.

I asked for a one-on-one meeting with Meg, as we'd only met once. Who would be the parent now? Would it still be fifty-fifty with just David and me? Or would it be the three of us equally? What exactly would be her new role in my family? I was afraid I would be losing my role as the only mother, especially for my daughter. The mother-daughter relationship was one that I had always dreamed of, the one I never had with my mother. Sienna's new "stepmom" might jeopardize this. I wanted to be the one to take my daughter to buy her first bra, and to be there for her when she'll have her first period or her first heartbreak. I was afraid I would miss those moments.

I talked with Meg, and while neither of us had the answers, we left each other understanding and believing that love was going to guide us. She reassured me that the wellbeing of my children was one of her top priorities. She'd been supportive and I trust that she will continue. I might not completely agree with them moving into a new house so quickly, but again, it's not my life anymore. All I could—and can—do is try to make sure that our relationship stays as good as it has been so far, and that we work together.

Meg has been a great influence on my ex-husband, and I love the fact that we share many of the same family values. She is good for David; she is good for my kids, and is very good to me. I left our meeting knowing that everything would be okay. We'd made sure of it, together.

Just a few days later, Sienna asked, "If Dad and Meg get married, will I have to call her Mom?" I've been thinking about this since his first girlfriend. What if my kids wanted to call her "Mom"? I asked friends and family for advice. Most of the feedback I got was, "Hell No!" or "They can't do that!" or "You can't allow this. You're the mom, not her." But I thought: Does it really matter? It's just a name. As long as they are not being forced to, if they want to call her Mom or give her a mother's day present, who am I to tell them no? They love me just the same. And if it brings more love to her and to my children, what's wrong with that?

I told Sienna that if they got married, Meg would become her daddy's wife, not her mom. Just like Daddy would become Meg's husband, not the daddy of her kids. I also told her that she could call Meg mom if she wanted to and that it would not change the love I have for her. She seemed relieved.

A month or so after the move, Liam turned eleven. I began preparing for his party. I asked David if Meg was going to join. He told me that she is a part of him; whenever I wanted him to be somewhere, she was going to be there too, and to please include her in every family event. I promised him I would. We now share a calendar for the children, so she knows what's going on, and can be part of our lives. When they need to take a few days off to vacation, I take the children, and vice versa. We celebrated Christmas together with a lovely dinner, and presents. She is part of the family, and so is her daughter, who lives with them half the time.

My relationship with David has strengthened in some ways and has lessened in others. We have more respect for each other today than before, and I am definitely less present in their daily lives. We know that we will always be there to support each other. We want happiness for each other, and Meg understands that.

I am lucky to have her as my ex-husband's new partner, as she improves the quality of our relationship. Seeing other divorced couples fighting (or just the remembrance of his past relationship), helps us realize that what we have built should be cherished. We both feel fortunate for the life we have, which David acknowledges me for. He regularly thanks me for holding onto the torch of this vision, and for being the driver of this beautiful divorce. We are now in maintenance mode; the hard work has been done, and the foundation is strong.

The children have also found their rhythm, and are enjoying their new house. They text me during the week to ask me who's taking them to soccer or the orthodontist. Sienna stills needs me when she is with her daddy. When she is sad, I text David after our call to give her a big hug. It's not about me telling him what to do, but me telling him what our children need, and he is very receptive. In the end, it only makes us better parents.

Of course, from time to time, there are some mishaps, but nothing we haven't been able to manage. We learn as we go, always with the same goal in mind: A happy life for all of us.

# Chapter Nineteen

# When Is The Right Time For A New Relationship?

David has settled down and is now a couple. I always thought that I too would find another man quickly. But when I became single, I found that I was not in a hurry for another relationship. I first needed to figure out who I was and who I'd become. I have changed a lot since the last time I was on my own, almost twenty years ago. I needed to know whether I liked certain things because my ex-husband liked them, or because we liked them, or if I actually liked them? I went through the first few months of my single life getting reacquainted with myself.

I took this time to assess and understand what went wrong in my marriage, what my part was, and what I wanted or needed to change for a future relationship. I took an honest look at what I was doing and who I was being during our marriage.

I also wanted to focus on my children and our relationship without their dad living with us. Before I could think about bringing a new man into the mix, I wanted them to feel secure, safe, and loved. Between getting a new home, starting a new life, raising my children, and working on my relationship with my ex-husband, I did not have the energy, time or desire to meet someone new.

About six months after the divorce, I thought it might be time, and went on a few dates. But very quickly I realized I still was not ready. Before I could think about being serious with another man, I had to understand the true meaning of a healthy relationship. I started to observe and ask questions of married couples that seemed to have it together. I wanted to know what made their marriage thrive, and I learned that what may be working for them would not necessarily work for me. I had to create my own definition of a healthy relationship.

After lengthy consideration, I came up with a list of what was important and crucial to me. The first and main characteristic of a beautiful and healthy relationship starts with respect. Respect, however, is such a big word that means different things to different people. For me, it is about listening and being heard by both partners; feeling secure enough to be vulnerable, knowing it will not be used against me in times of conflict; having him accept, without judgment; being appreciated and having my boundaries honored.

As I was feeling lonely and wanted to be loved, I put myself out there again. I tried Tinder and Match.com. I met a few men (some of them became good friends), but most were uninteresting and quite boring to me. After a few dates, I removed myself from the dating scene to focus on me, again. I still wasn't sure what I was looking for, or who I wanted to let in my life. Yet I did want to fall in love again, and wanted someone to love me. What should be relatively easy and natural, was very complicated. I had my kids half the time, which meant that the man had to fit my schedule. I eventually did meet someone I liked, and after a few weeks decided to tell my children. They met him and were okay with him. They'd already met my ex-husband's first girlfriend, and I wanted them to see that I too, could be happy. Sadly, the relationship did not work. After that, I decided I was not going to bring anyone home to meet my children, unless I truly believed he was the one.

I hadn't found the perfect man, so I started a "wish list" of attributes, important to me, and for my man. I was now forty-five years old, and would no longer look for potential. I didn't have another twenty years to give to a man who hadn't worked out his life. I realized that if a person that age hadn't reached it, there was little chance he ever would. I have been told that women see the potential in men, and hope that he will reach it. It might have been true when I was in my twenties, but now, I was about the present. What was that person doing and who was he being right now? It was no longer about potential, but reality.

My "attribute list" helped me be decisive, and I recognized that physical traits are not as important as who the person is or behaves. I wanted someone who lived life to the fullest, who loved to travel, who was in good shape (which is a lifestyle rather than a physical attribute), who was kind, funny, supportive, interesting and an amazing lover. One evening, at a girlfriend's dinner, with mostly married women, I was asked if I was seeing anyone. Upon saying no, they asked if I had a list. Yes I did, to which one of them replied, that it should be narrowed and I was too picky. That was the silliest idea ever. Why would I bring my expectations down when I know what is important to me? So, no, I was not going to ask for less. It might take longer to find the right person, but I was not going to settle for less.

This list might change over time, but for now, it gives me clarity about how I want my life to be and who I want to include in it, be it boyfriends, or just friends. As a dear friend of mine would say, we are who we surround ourselves with.

I can see myself in another long-term relationship that works. For that to happen, I need to give myself time to find the person who fits the bill. And for now, Mr. Right will have to wait. My children and I come first.

Long term relationship or not, I believe that joy is very important to live happily. There is no guarantee of happiness. Is it going to last or not? Who knows, but it is important to grab it when it shows up and enjoy it. I wanted my children to understand that, so I allowed myself to feel joy no matter what might be the outcome. I fell in love and got crushed twice. For those brief periods, my heart was singing, and my life was so colorful. I do not regret anything.

# Chapter Twenty

## The Aftermath

I keep hearing people say, "It takes time to be okay after a divorce; it takes time to let go; it takes time to be civil with your ex." It seems, that this is the answer for everything. Time will heal. But here is the truth: Time doesn't heal; it only makes you forget.

Then why does it take some of us one year to completely be at peace, and move forward on a strong path, while others are back in court fighting, five years later. And others still need twenty years to have a civil conversation?

While time helps numb the pain, it doesn't necessarily help us to work through it. It only helps us forget about it for a while (until the heart decides to bring it up again).

I read this one day: "Imagine yourself driving and you get a flat. You stop the car, get out and inspect it. You have no spare. You can stare at the flat all day, and hope it refills itself. Or, you realize the tire needs changing, call AAA, and you're on your way".

When a difficult situation arises, it's important to get support. The better the support, the faster the recovery. I can wait to see if my heart and head will be sane again, or I can get the help I need to arrive at my happy place. A Beautiful Divorce is about taking the first step to reach your destination, faster.

It's good to look back occasionally, to appreciate what we've built, from where we've come, and what we've achieved. I had days, when creating this new relationship seemed hopeless. But we kept at it, and here we are. For all of you in transition, I wish you courage to hold the torch of your vision, and to work through difficult times, to make it happen. A Beautiful Divorce is possible—and it's worth it!

It took a divorce to finally understand how to deal with some of my ex-husband's shortcomings, and how to communicate with him. It works because I don't live with him anymore, and can leave when I don't want to be around him. I take the good and leave the rest.

As a result of my divorce, I now know better than ever who I am—my strengths, my shortcomings. I've discovered gratitude, and this is what I learned:

- To let go and build boundaries.
- The true meaning of respect.
- To be accountable.
- To ask for what I want and to stand my ground.
- To breathe.
- I do not respond to triggers as I once did.
- That much of what I blamed on my then husband, were really my issues.
- What a healthy relationship is.

I am now a stronger woman and a better person, and that's what I focus on.

The question I often ask myself, and am asked by others is: Was it worth it? If I could redo it all, would I still ask for a divorce? I am happier today than I was in the last years of our marriage. David is happier too. I see my children becoming the people I wanted them to be. So, yes, it was completely worth it.

Divorce has given me a second chance to live on my own terms, with the knowledge and wisdom I gained. I share a lot about the beautiful parts and the results of all the hard work, and I don't always go into the pain that he, his friends and family caused me. I do not talk about this in detail, out of fear of hurting someone, of being wrong, but mostly, because it could destroy what I've built.

It takes Herculean strength to end a relationship, and even more to have a *beautiful divorce*. Why not channel that pain for self-growth and to create something better, instead of suffering through it, as if you had no choice? When I view my life, I forget the pain it took me to get here. I see the happiness surrounding us, and most of all, the gratitude. It's a long road, but the view from here is amazing.

# Chapter Twenty-one

## Random Raw Truths

- We still trigger each other as when we were married if left together for too long. The difference is that I can now turn around with a smile and say, okay, I will see you later, and not have to deal with it every day.

- We still argue from time to time. We are the same people; I am just learning to respond to it differently.

- I am a mother a hundred percent of the time, even if it's not my week with the kids. Yet I also love the free time that I haven't had since the birth to my first son.

- I learned that it is hard to let go of the pain that friends and family inflict, with their judgments and comments.

- I miss not seeing half of my kids' lives.

- I email or text David regularly to praise him, for being a good daddy, a good person, and a good ex-husband. I send him pictures of the kids, so he does not miss the moments away from them.

- When I got a cancer scare, three years after the divorce, he was the first one I called. He is still my go-to person when big things happen. I share the good news and bad news.

- I still get mad and sometimes react too quickly, especially when I am not feeling included in my family.

- Divorce is forever, there is no exit, so I better make it work.

- I learned that it's not always easy to be the girlfriend or boyfriend of a beautifully divorced couple. Jealousy gets in the way. You have to be extremely self-confident, loving and understanding. Seeing your loved one having a relationship with someone else, and sharing children, can be difficult at times.

- If I had to divorce all over again, I would.

- Litigation lawyers scare the heck out of me and I don't want to be near them.

- I enjoy seeing people being puzzled when they see David and me together, especially when Meg comes along. It blows their minds.

- I miss the bike rides David and I had right after our divorce. I understand why we don't have them anymore, but it was a nice way to connect and talk about the kids. Now, we do that over lunch sometimes, but mostly via text and emails, which is more businesslike.

- I am grateful that he chose Meg as his partner. She is an important ingredient in the balance and happiness of my life. If she was not his partner, I would want to have her as a friend.

- I would not go see a therapist to help navigate the challenges of divorce, if that person had never been married or never had children.

- I am grateful to have the ability to forget bad things and remember only the good.

- I am thankful for all that I have learned from my ex-husband. Now that I have started my own company (www.BeautifulDivorce.com), I realize how much knowledge I gained during those sixteen years of marriage. I learned from the best.

- Even after the divorce, I still needed my ex-husband's approval, for a long time. I am learning to disentangle myself from him, get stronger and be my own person.

- I am a much happier person. I still have moments of deep sadness and loneliness, but I am mostly living my life in a positive and joyful way.

- No matter how beautiful the divorce, kids are affected. It changes their dreams, too. The separation shapes their fears, their strengths, their values, what they believe and who they are. And each one reacts differently. Flexibility, patience, and understanding are key to support them.

- I learned a lot about relationship and leadership by dancing Tango. I learned what it meant to be in a healthy relationship, what the other gives and receives, and how you lead and follow in a natural way.

- I discovered that I am a complex woman. I strive to be better all the time. I am filled with emotions, so it must not have been easy to be my husband. While I have my share of complaints about my ex, I bow to him for living with me for sixteen years.

- It was very hard to write this book. I relived emotions that brought me back to the pain. It was extremely therapeutic, but I cried a lot.

- I wish that I could have written more about the fun times and the happiness, since my divorce, to really show how beautiful life has become.

- The upside of having my kids half the time: (although I miss them) I don't have to cook if I choose not to; I eat when I want; I only have to pick up after myself; and I love the sweet sound of silence.

- I love my life.

===

I would like to thank you for reading my journey.

Please share the love, and pass this book on to a friend, a family member, or anyone else who might need it, or tell them to visit www.BeautifulDivorce.com


Thank you again. I wish you love, joy, and courage.

Sandrine

=========================================================

*Read on to Questions and Answers...*

# Questions and Answers

(from Friends, Family, Acquaintances and Strangers)

**Q: What do you do to create beauty when there's no reciprocal respect?**

A: There are two cases:

1) You want a Beautiful Divorce, but the other party doesn't. You can't control what the other will say or do, but you can control yourself. Teach your children what you want them to be through your actions.

Do you want them to respect their spouse or parents when they grow up? Then show them how to do it. No, your partner may not do the same, and that's okay. You're creating the environment you want for your children. What are your values? What do you want to instill in them? You don't know what your kids will learn, but you're giving them a choice. If you are kind and respectful to your ex-spouse, you may be pleasantly surprised how the other party reacts. If it doesn't come back the way you would like, then at least you know that you are being the person you want your children to be.

2) You can't stand your partner and you want a Beautiful Divorce, but don't know how to do it? Nothing to like about your partner? Then hold on to this: Remember, she or he is the other parent. They are the co-creator of what you love the most. And they deserve respect for that. You only need one thing to hold onto. Find it!!! What do you want your kids to learn? Right now, they're learning from everything you are and do, not so much what you say. It's time to take a good look at who and what you're choosing to be and make the necessary changes to be the best example for them.

After all, we keep saying our kids are the most precious thing we have and that we would die for them? Then, owe respect to the other parent for giving us our most precious treasure. Beautiful Divorce starts with the kids. Pack the hate into a suitcase and leave it behind. Not easy? Nope!! Still thinking your kids are your priority? Then do this for them.

**Q: I feel my ex-spouse uses the kids against me. What do I do about it?**

A: Focus on what you're doing and who you want to be. If you focus on what your ex is saying or doing, it will drive you crazy, and you'll end up putting your kids in the middle. Who do you want them to become? Be that person, even on the difficult days. If the kids report something their dad said about you, just breathe, smile, and move on. Or you can say something like, "I'm sorry he feels this way." And then move on. Kids are not stupid; they understand what's going on. Be the better person. Be the adult. Don't put your kids in the middle. Most of us say we don't, but sadly, we do.

**Q: Do you think therapy helps keep marriages together?**

A: The fact is, fifty percent of marriages fail, no matter how much therapy you do. This statistic has been the same for many years and nothing seems to bring it down. For a relationship to work, both spouses need to want it, and must be ready to do the hard work. What I find missing from many types of therapy, is the lack of commitment to a healthy relationship— and the vision of a beautiful married life. We spend too much time blaming the other instead of understanding our own issues and needs. Therapy is not the only way to get help. I would also suggest looking at relationship coaching.

**Q: So the STBX (soon to be ex) and I agreed that he would claim the kids on our taxes, and he would give me more than half. Well, he informed me that he's keeping it all. The court order says he has to give me seventy-percent. I'm afraid I'll say the wrong thing out of anger and make the situation worse.**

A: I would write him a note:
"Bob, a while ago, we agreed that you would declare the kids on the taxes and give me half of the tax refund. Despite the court's declaration that I should receive seventy-percent, I thought we agreed that a fifty-fifty split between us would be more than fair to you. However, now you're telling me that you don't agree with our arrangement. I'm not sure what happened that changed your mind. I'm not looking for a fight. I want to understand where that leaves me and in what direction we need to go. I do want us to work together, and I want to hear your side. So, that I understand your current position, and we can decide what to do together. Being angry at each other would only cost us time, money, bitterness, resentment, and more pain. Let's try to find the best solution for all of

us, and mostly, what would be best for the kids. Let's make it a win-win. What do you say?

Thank you, Susane."

I like to keep the facts straight. I wouldn't say, "You lied to me again; I can never trust you; you always fall short..." and so on. Every time I write a note, I ask myself if this is going to take me on the road to the Beautiful Divorce or the ugly one? I always look for a solution that makes us all winners. While there's so much anger, it's important to see that this is only because we're hurting. In this case, we avoid the ugly path by first trying to understand the situation before assuming the worst of our ex. We're making a conscious effort not to bring up all the bad things each of us did during the marriage. We ended the marriage to have a better life. Show him how to become partners in the pursuit of happiness. His answer might not be what you want to hear. But just stay calm. You can always stay calm. No finger pointing. Maintain healthy boundaries. If the conversation evolves into name-calling or agressivity, then just say "I am sorry you feel this way", remove yourself, and let your partner know that you can talk about it later when you both can communicate respectfully. It works!!!!

Some feedback I got:

"I'm right there with you! Hard work at first but SOOOO worth the effort."

"We're better friends and co-parents now than when we were married. Many people think our relationship is weird because we help each other. But I'm grateful for who we are now."

"This is an amazing perspective and my son's dad and I are working hard on achieving a 'Beautiful Divorce' for the sake of our son and each other."

"Sharing makes a difference. It does give a new perspective and helps people get into action. Thank you for your support!!"

"I now take the time to think, without rushing to a nasty response, and say to myself, 'Be nice!' It's working, and he's being nicer in return, so the kids are really benefiting. Life is much easier this way for everyone involved."

**Q: How do I keep calm when my ex wants to fight?**

A: No matter how well your divorce goes, there will always be triggers that will take you to the edge. Knowing that those moments are coming, helps prepare for them. Understand that the person who is angry and looking for a fight is only expressing his hurt and pain. Reacting to that only makes the situation worse. Learn to breath and take a step back. Have a plan of action prepared just in case. For example: "I can see that you're angry. Why don't we talk later?" This will allow you some time to let things cool off, and once everything is calm, you can attempt your conversation again. I have to admit that while I work very hard to be calm and collected, I haven't always been. I have triggers just like everyone else, and there were times I became the angry bear. I'm very fortunate that my ex could recognize that and would work to calm me down. He, too, now understands that reacting and fighting only makes the situation worse for everyone. We don't necessarily cave, but rather, just work to find a solution that we can both agree on.

**Q: If you want to get along with him, won't he walk all over you?**

A: That couldn't be further from the truth. People often believe that if a divorced couple is getting along and working together, that one of them is being taken advantage of. A Beautiful Divorce is about growing, finding your strengths and your own way to create a glorious life. Being a victim is not part of this plan. Learn to choose your battles. That means letting go of a lot of them. Stand up for what's important to you, and what you need. A fight does not mean you have to be nasty. It just means that you're creating your own boundaries. Make sure that the long-term consequences are in alignment with your life commitment. It's not about showing who's right or wrong. It's about building a new foundation based on values you now want to create for your new life.

Q: **When going through a separation or divorce, how do the children cope? My kids' father and I are finally separating after eight years. Our oldest son is three, our daughter is one, and we have a six-month-old daughter. I'm so worried for the two oldest. My husband has been a very hands-on father. The kids absolutely adore him, and he's been at home with them since the oldest was one. He'll be moving out of state, which makes things even worse, as he'll be absent in their life for months at a time. Any advice on what to expect and how to deal with it?**

A: First, it's essential that your children know that you and your ex-husband are still a family and that you're still their parents. Their wellbeing is essential. Communication between the two of you will change. It's essential to talk about their dad regularly, in a beautiful way. They love their daddy, and your role as a mom is to make sure their relationship grows strong. It's about learning to be supportive of each other so you can both be amazing parents. It's about listening to the children and giving them what they need. Also, I highly recommend seeing a child play therapist. The children don't always have the words to express what they feel, and usually they keep it all in. Sometimes, we're so blinded by our emotions, that we can't see where we're going and what we're doing. And lastly, I would recommend to have as many video calls as possible, anytime your ex-husband or your children want. This helps them grow together, but apart.

**Q: How did you keep sane and calm during the divorce?**

A: I felt overwhelmed by everything during the divorce process. It was like being in shock, where you see everything, in slow motion, and nothing makes sense; we hear, but don't fully register.

My divorce started with anger, finger pointing, and hurtful words. I turned to meditation to center myself through the difficult conversations and to let go of emotions that ensued. I couldn't wait to fall asleep, so I could forget what was happening. An eight-hour break from reality. I could not stop thinking about the divorce. Guided meditation calmed my mind, and helped me sleep. If I woke in the middle of the night, with a racing mind, I would listen to the sweet voice of this English man telling me to let go, and to dream of beautiful English gardens.

I also signed up for a self-defense class called Krav Maga. It provided me a safe place to unleash. I kicked, punched and screamed out all my anger! That's how I stayed sane that first year.

**Q: It seems that you still care a lot about your ex husband, shouldn't you run back to him, or learn how to be divorced?**

A: Why can't we truly believe in a divorce where we still want the best for each other?

Why are people so eager to make my Beautiful Divorce something other than what it is? The too typical divorce involves blame and "hate" toward each other for years, while, placing the kids in the middle, in harm's way.

My divorce has become one of the healthiest relationships I've ever had. And my dream of caring and supporting each other, and raising our children as a team, also came true!

Does it mean I want to run back to him, and be his wife? No. We tried for sixteen years. So here's my answer: We didn't know how to be married, but we sure know how to be divorced!

**Q: How do you know if your kids are doing well with the divorce?**

A: When we decided to divorce, we went to see a child therapist; first to ask how to tell the children, and saw another therapist for the children. I wanted to make sure we were following them closely.

While I have no idea what they'll remember in ten, twenty, or thirty years, and what truth they'll create, I can report what I see (facts) and what I sense (mother's intuition). What I see is that they're excelling in school, there are fewer crises, and everyone seems to have found peace within. They've even told us they can tell we're happier now, and are glad we chose to divorce. After several years of listening, talking, asking questions, and caring for them, they know the love from their mom and dad hasn't changed.

When something happens concerning one of the children, we communicate about it. We divorced each other, but NOT the family.

**Q: I had a mother tell me that her ex was bringing his new girlfriend for a weekend stay with him and her**

**children. She said, "I can't express how sick I feel. I'm completely crushed. I hate this so much! Why?"**

A: It's hard to have another woman around your kids; however, you need to be conscious of what you wish for them. Do you want this new woman to hate your children, and them to hate her? Or do you want your little ones to be loved, and to learn how to love, as well? It will be one of the hardest lessons to give: Love and respect the person you want to hate the most. It's a beautiful life lesson to teach them. And most of all, you're showing them that they're worthy of being loved, no matter from where the love comes.

Eventually, for the wellbeing of the children, we became a team of three. It's not easy, and we've had a few bumps in the road. But one thing is always sure: we all want to love them. Their happiness has always been our first commitment.

I told this woman, "Of course, you're feeling sick. This hurts the deepest. Having the perfect family is a dream you've had since you were a little girl, and now it's gone. Allow yourself the grief and the sadness, but never lose sight of the love for your children. Please, wish them a great time together, allow them to love, and to be loved."

41687423R00120

Made in the USA
Middletown, DE
11 April 2019